Mmmm...
Chocolate

Mmmm... Chocolate

This edition published in 2011

LOVE FOOD is an imprint of Parragon Books Ltd

Parragon
Queen Street House
4 Queen Street
Bath BA1 1HE, UK

ISBN: 978-1-4454-2787-4

Printed in China

Design by Talking Design
Cover photography by Charlie Richards
Cover image styled by Mary Wall
Introduction by Linda Doeser

Notes for the Reader
This book uses both metric and imperial measurements. Follow the same units of measurement throughout; do not mix metric and imperial. All spoon measurements are level: teaspoons are assumed to be 5 ml, and tablespoons are assumed to be 15 ml. Unless otherwise stated, milk is assumed to be full fat, eggs and individual vegetables are medium, and pepper is freshly ground black pepper.

The times given are an approximate guide only. Preparation times differ according to the techniques used by different people and the cooking times may also vary from those given. Optional ingredients, variations or serving suggestions have not been included in the calculations.

Recipes using raw or very lightly cooked eggs should be avoided by infants, the elderly, pregnant women, convalescents and anyone suffering from an illness. Pregnant and breastfeeding women are advised to avoid eating peanuts and peanut products. Sufferers from nut allergies should be aware that some of the ready-made ingredients used in the recipes in this book may contain nuts. Always check the packaging before use.

contents

introduction

For many people, chocolate is right at the top of their list of favourite foodstuffs. Its sweet richness combined with its literally melt-in-the-mouth texture always make it a special treat. We give chocolates as birthday and anniversary gifts, make chocolate cakes for celebrations, impress our dinner guests with lavish chocolate desserts, boost our flagging energy in the mid-morning with a chocolate cookie or gooey muffin and soothe our souls at bedtime with a steaming mug of hot chocolate.

types of chocolate

Basically, chocolate is a mixture of cocoa and sugar, although other ingredients, such as milk, honey and ginger, may be added. There are many different types of cocoa beans – the seeds of the cacao tree – ranging in colour from almost black to light brown and in flavour from mild to bitter. Whether ordinary or fine, the beans undergo a lengthy process of cleaning, roasting, cracking and grinding to produce chocolate liquor which then may be transformed into cocoa butter for making chocolate or into cocoa powder.

The proportion of cocoa liquor to sugar determines the type of chocolate and the higher the ratio, the darker and more bitter the final result. The quality and type of the beans and the percentage of cocoa butter, as well as the care and expertise expended in its preparation, determine the quality of the chocolate. Price is often an indication of quality but you can also tell by the chocolate's appearance, texture and taste. Good quality chocolate is shiny brown with no lumps, air holes or specks and should snap cleanly when broken. It melts on

the tongue releasing a rich chocolate flavour rather than the taste of cocoa and the 'mouth feel' should be neither sticky nor greasy.

PLAIN CHOCOLATE is dark, lightly sweetened and should contain at least 50 per cent cocoa solids (check the label).

DARK CHOCOLATE is similar to plain chocolate, but more bitter with a very rich flavour.

MILK CHOCOLATE is made with the addition of milk solids and is lighter in colour, sweeter and milder in flavour than plain or dark chocolate.

WHITE CHOCOLATE is made from sweetened cocoa butter and, strictly speaking, is not chocolate at all. Technically, it is white confectionery coating but most people call it white chocolate. Use it only in recipes that specify white chocolate as it cannot be substituted for plain, dark or milk chocolate.

CHOCOLATE COUVERTURE is simply very high quality plain or dark chocolate with a high cocoa butter content. Milk chocolate couverture is also available. It is widely used in the confectionery industry and by professional chefs for baking and making icings, sauces and mousses. It is quite tricky to handle and is not essential for most home baking.

COCOA POWDER, used for flavouring drinks, is unsweetened and has a strong flavour. It is widely used in baking.

DRINKING CHOCOLATE is a mixture of cocoa powder and sugar. It is mild in flavour, sweet and best kept for making drinks. As a general rule, it is not suitable for baking and cannot be used as a substitute for cocoa powder.

top tips for cooking with chocolate

- Chocolate is best stored in a cool place rather than the refrigerator, where it can become tainted with the smell of other foods and acquire a bloom on the surface. This is not harmful but does spoil its appearance.

- Never melt chocolate on its own in a saucepan over direct heat as it scorches easily. However, it can be melted over a very low heat if it is combined with other ingredients such as butter, cream, milk or coffee. Stir occasionally and remove from the heat as soon as the chocolate has melted and the mixture is smooth.

- To melt chocolate on its own, break it into small pieces and put them into a heatproof bowl. Set the bowl over a pan of gently simmering water, making sure that the base of the bowl does not touch the surface of the water. Heat gently, stirring occasionally, until the chocolate has melted and is smooth, then remove from the heat. If melting white chocolate, chill it first, then grate finely into the bowl before heating.

- If steam gets into the chocolate when you are melting it over simmering water, it is likely to solidify or seize. Stirring in 1 teaspoon of vegetable fat or grapeseed oil for every 25 g/1 oz chocolate will rectify the problem. The chocolate can then be used for baking or making desserts but is not suitable for making decorations, such as curls or leaves. This method does not work on seized white chocolate.

- To melt chocolate in the microwave, break it into small pieces and put them into a microwave-safe bowl. Don't cover the bowl and heat on Medium for 30 seconds, then stir and check whether it has melted. Continue heating, stirring and checking at 10-second intervals until the chocolate is smooth. You cannot tell whether it has melted simply by looking as it will hold its shape even when melted. White chocolate should be chilled before melting, finely grated, then heated on Low and checked frequently in the same way.

- An easy way to make chocolate curls is to shave the edge of a firm chocolate bar with a vegetable peeler. For a more professional decoration spread a thin layer of melted chocolate on a marble slab or chilled baking sheet and leave until just set. Holding a metal spatula or palette knife at a low angle, scrape the chocolate into long curls or scrolls.

- To make chocolate leaves, use firm, clean shiny leaves with short stems, such as rose leaves. Brush the shiny side of the leaves with melted chocolate using a small paintbrush and leave to set on a baking sheet lined with greaseproof paper in a cool place. When the chocolate has set, carefully pull off the leaves by holding the stems.

Mmmm...
cakes

chocolate fudge cake

serves 8

- 175 g/6 oz unsalted butter, softened, plus extra for greasing
- 55 g/2 oz plain chocolate
- 2 tbsp milk
- 175 g/6 oz plain white flour
- 1 tbsp baking powder
- 175 g/6 oz dark muscovado sugar
- 3 eggs, beaten
- 1 tsp vanilla extract
- milk chocolate curls or grated chocolate, to decorate

frosting

- 100 g/3½ oz plain chocolate
- 55 g/2 oz unsalted butter, softened
- 175 g/6 oz icing sugar
- 1 tsp vanilla extract
- 1 tbsp milk

1 Preheat the oven to 180°C/350°F/Gas Mark 4. Grease and line a 23-cm/9-inch round cake tin. Place the chocolate and milk in a small pan and heat gently until melted, without boiling. Remove from the heat. Sift the flour and baking powder into a large bowl and add the butter, muscovado sugar, eggs and vanilla extract. Beat well until smooth, then stir in the melted chocolate mixture, mixing evenly.

2 Spoon the mixture into the prepared tin and smooth the top level. Bake in the preheated oven for 50–60 minutes, until firm to the touch and just beginning to shrink away from the sides of the tin. Leave to cool in the tin for 10 minutes, then turn out and finish cooling on a wire rack. When cold, carefully slice the cake horizontally into two layers.

3 To make the frosting, melt the chocolate with the butter in a small pan over a low heat. Remove from the heat and stir in the icing sugar, vanilla extract and milk, then beat well until smooth. Sandwich the cake layers together with half the frosting, then spread the remainder on top of the cake, swirling with a palette knife. Decorate with chocolate curls.

chocolate ganache cake

serves 10

- 175 g/6 oz butter, plus extra for greasing
- 175 g/6 oz caster sugar
- 4 eggs, beaten
- 250 g/9 oz self-raising flour
- 1 tbsp cocoa powder
- 50 g/1¾ oz plain chocolate, melted
- 200 g/7 oz chocolate-flavoured cake covering

ganache

- 450 ml/16 fl oz cream
- 375 g/13 oz plain chocolate, broken into pieces

1 Preheat the oven to 180°C/350°F/Gas Mark 4. Grease and line a 20-cm/8-inch springform cake tin. Beat the butter and sugar until light and fluffy. Gradually add the eggs, beating well after each addition. Sift the flour and cocoa powder together and fold into the cake mixture. Fold in the melted chocolate.

2 Pour into the prepared tin and smooth the top. Bake in the preheated oven for 40 minutes, or until springy to the touch. Leave to cool in the tin for 10 minutes, then turn out and finish cooling on a wire rack. When cold, carefully slice the cake horizontally into two layers.

3 To make the ganache, place the cream in a saucepan and bring to the boil, stirring. Add the chocolate and stir until melted. Pour into a bowl, cool, then chill for 2 hours, or until set and firm. Whisk the mixture until light and fluffy. Reserve one-third of the ganache. Use the remaining ganache to sandwich the cake together and spread over the top and sides of the cake.

4 Melt the cake covering and spread it over a large sheet of baking paper. Leave to cool until just set. Cut into strips a little wider than the height of the cake. Place the strips around the edge of the cake, overlapping them slightly. Pipe the reserved ganache in tear drops to cover the top of the cake. Leave to chill for 1 hour.

chocolate cake with syrup

serves 12

- 115 g/4 oz butter, plus extra for greasing
- 225 g/8 oz plain chocolate, broken into pieces
- 1 tbsp strong black coffee
- 4 eggs
- 2 egg yolks
- 115 g/4 oz caster sugar
- 40 g/1½ oz plain flour
- 2 tsp ground cinnamon
- 85 g/3 oz ground almonds
- chocolate-covered coffee beans, to decorate

syrup

- 300 ml/10 fl oz strong black coffee
- 115 g/4 oz caster sugar
- 1 cinnamon stick

1 Preheat the oven to 190°C/375°F/Gas Mark 5. Grease and line a 20-cm/8-inch round cake tin. Place the chocolate, butter and coffee in a heatproof bowl and set over a saucepan of gently simmering water until melted. Stir to blend, then remove from the heat and leave to cool slightly.

2 Place the whole eggs, egg yolks and sugar in a separate bowl and whisk together until thick and pale. Sift the flour and cinnamon over the egg mixture. Add the almonds and the chocolate mixture and fold in carefully. Spoon the mixture into the prepared tin. Bake in the preheated oven for 35 minutes, or until a skewer inserted into the centre comes out clean. Leave to cool in the tin for 5 minutes, then turn out and finish cooling on a wire rack.

3 Meanwhile, make the syrup. Place the coffee, sugar and cinnamon stick in a heavy-based saucepan and heat gently, stirring, until the sugar has dissolved. Increase the heat and boil for 5 minutes, or until reduced and thickened slightly. Keep warm. Pierce the surface of the cake with a cocktail stick, then drizzle over half the coffee syrup. Decorate with chocolate-covered coffee beans and serve with the remaining coffee syrup.

chocolate gâteau

serves 10
- 225 g/8 oz butter, softened, plus extra for greasing
- 225 g/8 oz golden caster sugar
- 4 eggs, beaten
- 225 g/8 oz self-raising flour
- 55 g/2 oz cocoa powder
- a little milk (optional)

filling
- 250 ml/9 fl oz whipping cream
- 225 g/8 oz white chocolate, broken into pieces

icing
- 350 g/12 oz plain chocolate, broken into pieces
- 115 g/4 oz butter
- 100 ml/3½ fl oz double cream

to decorate
- 115 g/4 oz plain chocolate caraque
- 2 tsp icing sugar and cocoa powder, mixed

1 To make the filling, put the whipping cream in a saucepan and heat to almost boiling. Put the white chocolate in a food processor and chop. With the motor running, pour the hot cream through the feed tube and process for 10–15 seconds, until smooth. Transfer to a bowl, leave to cool, then cover with clingfilm and chill in the refrigerator for 2 hours, or until firm. Whisk until just starting to hold soft peaks.

2 Preheat the oven to 180°C/350°F/Gas Mark 4. Grease and line the base of a 20-cm/8-inch round deep cake tin. Put the butter and sugar in a bowl and beat until light and fluffy. Gradually beat in the eggs. Sift the flour and cocoa powder into a bowl, then fold into the mixture, adding milk, if necessary, to make a dropping consistency.

3 Spoon into the prepared tin and bake in the oven for 45–50 minutes, until a skewer inserted into the centre comes out clean. Leave to cool in the tin for 5 minutes, then turn out and finish cooling on a wire rack.

4 To make the icing, put the plain chocolate in a heatproof bowl set over a saucepan of gently simmering water until melted. Stir in the butter and double cream. Leave to cool, stirring occasionally.

5 Slice the cake horizontally into 3 layers. Sandwich the layers together with the white chocolate filling. Cover the top and sides of the cake with the icing and arrange the chocolate caraque over the top. Sift the mixed icing sugar and cocoa powder on top.

chocolate rum torte

serves 8

- 175 g/6 oz unsalted butter, softened, plus extra for greasing
- 70 g/2½ oz plain chocolate, broken into pieces
- 2 tbsp milk
- 175 g/6 oz plain white flour
- 1 tbsp baking powder
- 175 g/6 oz dark muscovado sugar
- 3 eggs, beaten
- 1 tsp vanilla extract
- milk chocolate curls or grated chocolate, to decorate

frosting

- 225 g/8 oz plain chocolate, broken into pieces
- 225 ml/8 fl oz double cream
- 2 tbsp dark rum

1 Preheat the oven to 180°C/350°F/Gas Mark 4. Grease and line 3 × 18-cm/7-inch sandwich cake tins.

2 Place the chocolate and milk in a small saucepan and heat gently, without boiling, until melted. Stir and remove from the heat.

3 Sift the flour and baking powder into a large bowl and add the butter, sugar, eggs and vanilla extract. Beat well until smooth, then stir in the chocolate mixture.

4 Divide the mixture between the prepared tins and bake in the preheated oven for 40 minutes, or until springy to the touch. Leave to cool in the tins for 5 minutes, then turn out and finish cooling on wire racks.

5 To make the frosting, melt the chocolate with the cream and rum in a small saucepan over a low heat. Remove from the heat and leave to cool, stirring occasionally, until it reaches a spreadable consistency.

6 Sandwich the cakes together with about a third of the frosting, then spread the remainder over the top and sides of the cake, swirling with a palette knife. Sprinkle with chocolate curls and leave to set.

chocolate brownie cake

serves 10

- 200 g/7 oz butter, plus extra for greasing
- 115 g/4 oz plain chocolate, broken into pieces
- 280 g/10 oz granulated sugar
- 115 g/4 oz light muscovado sugar
- 4 eggs, beaten
- 175 g/6 oz plain flour
- 1 tsp vanilla extract
- pinch of salt
- 75 g/2¾ oz dried cranberries
- 75 g/2¾ oz toasted flaked almonds, plus extra to decorate

icing

- 115 g/4 oz plain chocolate
- 25 g/1 oz butter
- 225 g/8 oz icing sugar
- 3–4 tbsp milk

1 Preheat the oven to 180°C/350°F/Gas Mark 4. Grease and line the bases of 2 x 18-cm/7-inch round cake tins.

2 Place the butter in a heavy-based saucepan and add the chocolate. Heat gently, stirring frequently until the mixture has melted. Remove from the heat and stir until smooth. Add the sugars, stir well, then leave to cool for 10 minutes.

3 Gradually add the eggs to the cooled chocolate mixture, beating well after each addition. Stir in the flour, vanilla extract and salt. Stir in the cranberries and flaked almonds, mix, then divide between the prepared cake tins. Bake in the preheated oven for 25–30 minutes, or until springy to the touch. Leave to cool in the tins for 5 minutes, then turn out and finish cooling on wire racks.

4 To make the icing, melt the chocolate and butter in a heavy-based saucepan and stir until smooth. Gradually beat in the icing sugar with enough milk to give a smooth spreading consistency. Use a little of the icing to sandwich the two cakes together, then spread the top and sides with the remainder, swirling the top to give a decorative effect. Sprinkle the flaked almonds over the top to decorate.

chocolate & walnut cake

serves 8

- 25 g/1 oz butter, melted, plus extra for greasing
- 4 eggs
- 125 g/4½ oz caster sugar
- 75 g/2¾ oz plain chocolate, broken into pieces
- 125 g/4½ oz plain flour
- 1 tbsp cocoa powder
- 115 g/4 oz walnuts, finely chopped
- walnut halves, to decorate

icing

- 75 g/2¾ oz plain chocolate, broken into pieces
- 115 g/4 oz butter
- 175 g/6 oz icing sugar
- 2 tbsp milk

1 Preheat the oven to 160°C/325°F/Gas Mark 3. Grease and line an 18-cm/7-inch round cake tin.

2 Place the eggs and caster sugar in a bowl and whisk with an electric whisk for 10 minutes, or until foamy and a trail is left when the whisk is dragged across the surface. Put the chocolate in a heatproof bowl set over a saucepan of gently simmering water until melted. Remove from the heat.

3 Sift the flour and cocoa powder together and fold into the egg and sugar mixture. Fold in the melted butter, melted chocolate and chopped walnuts. Pour into the prepared tin and bake in the preheated oven for 30–35 minutes, or until springy to the touch. Leave to cool in the tin for 5 minutes, then turn out and finish cooling on a wire rack.

4 To make the icing, melt the chocolate as above and leave to cool slightly. Beat together the butter, icing sugar and milk until the mixture is pale and fluffy. Whisk in the melted chocolate.

5 Cut the cake horizontally into 2 layers. Place the bottom half on a serving plate, spread with half the icing and put the other half on top. Spread the remaining icing over the top of the cake. Decorate with walnut halves and serve.

chocolate orange cake

serves 8–10
- 175 g/6 oz butter, softened, plus extra for greasing
- 2 small oranges
- 85 g/3 oz plain chocolate
- 250 g/9 oz self-raising flour
- 1½ tsp baking powder
- 200 g/7 oz caster sugar
- 3 eggs, beaten

topping
- 175 g/6 oz icing sugar
- 2 tbsp orange juice
- 55 g/2 oz plain chocolate, broken into pieces

1 Preheat the oven to 160°C/325°F/Gas Mark 3. Grease an 850-ml/1½-pint fluted or plain ring tin.

2 Grate the rind from one of the oranges and set aside. Pare the rind from the other orange and set aside. Cut the skin and pith from the oranges, then cut them into segments by cutting down between the membranes with a sharp knife. Chop the segments into small pieces, reserving as much juice as possible. Grate the chocolate coarsely.

3 Sift the flour and baking powder into a bowl. Add the butter, sugar, eggs, grated orange rind and any reserved juice. Beat until the mixture is smooth. Fold in the chopped oranges and grated chocolate. Spoon the mixture into the prepared tin and bake in the preheated oven for 40 minutes, or until well risen. Leave to cool in the tin for 5 minutes, then turn out and finish cooling on a wire rack.

4 To make the topping, sift the icing sugar into a bowl and stir in enough orange juice to make a coating consistency. Using a spoon, drizzle the icing over the cake. Put the chocolate in a heatproof bowl set over a saucepan of gently simmering water until melted. Drizzle the melted chocolate over the cake. Cut the reserved pared orange rind into thin strips and scatter over the cake. Leave to set before serving.

chocolate & cherry gâteau

serves 8

- 175 g/6 oz unsalted butter, softened, plus extra for greasing
- 150 g/5½ oz plain white flour
- 2 tbsp cocoa powder
- 1 tbsp baking powder
- 175 g/6 oz golden caster sugar
- 3 eggs, beaten
- 1 tsp vanilla extract
- 2 tbsp milk
- 3 tbsp kirsch or brandy (optional)
- grated chocolate and fresh whole cherries, to decorate

filling & topping

- 450 ml/16 fl oz double or whipping cream
- 2 tbsp icing sugar
- 225 g/8 oz fresh dark red cherries, stoned

1 Preheat the oven to 180°C/350°F/Gas Mark 4. Grease and line the bases of 2 × 20-cm/8-inch sandwich cake tins.

2 Sift the flour, cocoa powder and baking powder into a large bowl and add the butter, caster sugar, eggs and vanilla extract. Beat well until the mixture is smooth, then stir in the milk.

3 Leave to cool in the tins for 5 minutes, then turn out and finish cooing on wire racks.

4 When the cakes are cold, sprinkle with the kirsch, if using. To make the filling and topping, whip the cream with the icing sugar until thick, then spread about a third over the top of one of the cakes. Spread the cherries over the cream and place the second cake on top.

5 Spread the remaining cream over the top and sides of the cake and decorate with grated chocolate and fresh whole cherries.

chocolate madeira cake

serves 8-10

- 115 g/4 oz butter, softened, plus extra for greasing
- 55 g/2 oz self-raising flour
- 1 tsp baking powder
- 115 g/4 oz caster sugar
- 3 eggs, beaten
- 25 g/1 oz ground almonds
- 115 g/4 oz drinking chocolate powder
- icing sugar, sifted, for dusting

icing

- 225 g/8 oz icing sugar
- 1½ tbsp cocoa powder
- 2 tbsp butter
- 3–4 tbsp hot water

1 Preheat the oven to 180°C/350°F/Gas Mark 4. Grease and line the base of an 18-cm/7-inch round cake tin. Sift the flour and baking powder into a bowl and set aside.

2 Cream the butter with the sugar until light and fluffy, then gradually beat in the eggs, adding a little of the flour after each addition. When all the eggs have been added, stir in the remaining flour together with the ground almonds. Sift the drinking chocolate powder into the mixture and stir lightly.

3 Spoon the mixture into the prepared cake tin. Bake in the preheated oven for 50–55 minutes, or until a skewer inserted into the centre comes out clean. Leave to cool in the tin for 10 minutes, then turn out and finish cooling on a wire rack.

4 To make the icing, sift the icing sugar and cocoa powder together into a mixing bowl and make a hollow in the centre. Place the butter in the centre. Mix with with sufficient hot water to form a smooth spreadable icing. Coat the top and sides of the cake with icing, swirling it to give a decorative effect. Dust with icing sugar.

chocolate heart cake

serves 12

- 150 ml/5 fl oz sunflower oil, plus extra for greasing
- 175 g/6 oz self-raising flour
- 2 tsp baking powder
- 55 g/2 oz cocoa powder
- 3 eggs
- 140 g/5 oz light muscovado sugar
- 150 ml/5 fl oz single cream
- fresh mint sprigs, to decorate

filling & topping

- 225 g/8 oz plain chocolate
- 250 ml/9 fl oz double cream
- 3 tbsp seedless raspberry jam
- 200 g/7 oz fresh or frozen raspberries

1 Preheat the oven to 180°C/350°F/Gas Mark 4. Grease and line the base of a 20-cm/8-inch heart-shaped cake tin. Sift the flour, baking powder and cocoa powder into a large bowl. Beat the eggs with the sugar, oil and single cream. Make a well in the dry ingredients and add the egg mixture, then stir to mix thoroughly, beating to a smooth batter.

2 Pour the mixture into the prepared tin and bake in the preheated oven for 25–30 minutes, or until risen and firm to the touch. Leave to cool in the tin for 10 minutes, then turn out and finish cooling on a wire rack. To make the filling and topping, place the chocolate and double cream in a saucepan over a low heat and stir until melted. Remove from the heat and stir until the mixture cools slightly and begins to thicken.

3 Use a sharp knife to cut the cake in half horizontally. Spread the cut surface of each half with the raspberry jam, then top with about 3 tablespoons of the chocolate mixture. Scatter half the raspberries over the base and replace the top, pressing lightly. Spread the remaining chocolate mixture over the top and sides of the cake, swirling with a palette knife. Top with the remaining raspberries and decorate with mint sprigs.

chocolate &
vanilla cake

serves 8
- 70 g/2½ oz unsalted butter, plus extra for greasing
- 115 g/4 oz self-raising flour, plus extra for dusting
- 55 g/2 oz plain chocolate
- 3 tbsp milk
- 85 g/3 oz caster sugar
- 1 egg, beaten
- 3 tbsp soured cream
- ½ tsp baking powder
- ½ tsp vanilla extract

1 Preheat the oven to 160°C/325°F/Gas Mark 3. Grease and line the base of a 450-g/1-lb loaf tin. Dust a little flour around the inside of the tin, shaking out the excess.

2 Break up the chocolate, place in a small heatproof bowl with the milk and set over a saucepan of simmering water. Heat gently until just melted. Remove from the heat.

3 Cream together the butter and sugar until light and fluffy. Beat in the egg and soured cream. Sift the flour and baking powder over the mixture, then fold in lightly and evenly using a metal spoon.

4 Spoon half the mixture into a separate bowl and stir in the chocolate mixture. Add the vanilla extract to the plain mixture.

5 Spoon the chocolate and vanilla mixtures alternately into the prepared loaf tin, swirling lightly with a knife or skewer for a marbled effect. Bake in the preheated oven for 40–45 minutes, or until well risen and firm to the touch.

6 Leave to cool in the tin for 10 minutes, then turn out and finish cooling on a wire rack.

chocolate poppy seed cake

serves 4
pastry
- 140 g/5 oz butter, softened
- generous 3 tbsp caster sugar
- pinch of salt
- 1 egg
- 200 g/7 oz flour, plus extra for dusting

filling
- 140 g/5 oz ground poppy seeds
- 6 tbsp milk
- 115 g/4 oz granulated sugar
- 55 g/2 oz plain chocolate, grated
- 55 g/2 oz raisins
- 55 g/2 oz candied peel, chopped
- 55 g/2 oz blanched almonds, grated
- 1 egg, beaten
- 1 tbsp caster sugar
- 1 tbsp whole poppy seeds

1 To make the pastry, beat together the butter, sugar and salt, add the egg, then stir in the flour and just enough cold water to make a soft dough. Cover with clingfilm and chill in the refrigerator for 1 hour.

2 Preheat the oven to 160°C/325°F/Gas Mark 3. Meanwhile, to make the filling, place the poppy seeds and milk in a saucepan and simmer, stirring, for 2 minutes. Remove the pan from the heat and stir in the granulated sugar, chocolate, raisins, candied peel and almonds. Set aside 1 teaspoon of the beaten egg and beat the remainder into the mixture.

3 Roll the pastry out thinly on a lightly floured counter and cut 4 x 20-cm/8-inch circles. Place one circle in a 20-cm/8-inch loose-bottom tart pan and spread over one-third of the filling. Repeat the layers, finishing with the last pastry circle. Press the edges together very lightly, then make a hole in the centre with the handle of a wooden spoon.

4 Brush the cake with the reserved beaten egg, then sprinkle with the caster sugar and whole poppy seeds. Bake in the preheated oven for about 45 minutes. Serve warm or cold.

chocolate truffle torte

serves 10

sponge
- butter, for greasing
- 50 g/1¾ oz caster sugar
- 2 eggs
- 40 g/1¼ oz plain flour
- 25 g/1 oz cocoa powder
- 4 tbsp strong black coffee
- 2 tbsp brandy

truffle filling
- 600 ml/1 pint whipping cream
- 425 g/15 oz plain chocolate, broken into pieces

to decorate
- cocoa powder
- icing sugar

1 Preheat the oven to 220°C/425°F/Gas Mark 7. Grease and line a 23-cm/9-inch springform cake tin. Put the sugar and eggs in a heatproof bowl set over a saucepan of gently simmering water. Whisk together until pale and resembling the texture of mousse. Remove from the heat. Sift in the flour and cocoa powder and fold gently into the mixture. Pour into the prepared tin and bake in the preheated oven for 7–10 minutes, or until risen and firm to the touch. Leave to cool in the tin for 10 minutes, then turn out and finish cooling on a wire rack.

2 Wash and dry the tin and replace the cooled cake in the tin. Mix together the coffee and brandy and brush over the cake. To make the truffle filling, put the cream in a bowl and whisk until just holding very soft peaks. Put the chocolate in a heatproof bowl set over a saucepan of gently simmering water until melted. Remove from the heat. Carefully fold the cooled melted chocolate into the cream. Pour the chocolate mixture over the sponge. Chill until set.

3 To decorate the torte, sift cocoa powder over the top and remove carefully from the tin. Using strips of card or baking paper, sift bands of icing sugar over the torte to create a striped pattern. Serve.

mocha layer cake

serves 8
- butter, for greasing
- 250 g/9 oz self-raising flour
- ¼ tsp baking powder
- 4 tbsp cocoa powder
- 115 g/4 oz caster sugar
- 2 eggs
- 2 tbsp golden syrup
- 150 ml/5 fl oz sunflower oil
- 150 ml/5 fl oz milk

filling
- 1 tsp instant coffee powder
- 1 tbsp boiling water
- 300 ml/10 fl oz
  double cream
- 2 tbsp icing sugar

to decorate
- 50 g/1¾ oz chocolate
  shavings
- 75 g marbled chocolate
  caraque
- icing sugar, sifted, for dusting

1 Preheat the oven to 180°C/350°F/Gas Mark 4. Lightly grease 3 × 18-cm/7-inch sandwich tins.

2 Sift the flour, baking powder and cocoa powder into a large mixing bowl. Stir in the sugar. Make a well in the centre and stir in the eggs, syrup, oil and milk. Beat with a wooden spoon, gradually mixing in the dry ingredients to make a smooth mixture. Divide the mixture between the prepared tins.

3 Bake in the preheated oven for 35–45 minutes, or until springy to the touch. Leave the cakes to cool in their tins for 5 minutes, then turn out and finish cooling on wire racks.

4 To make the filling, dissolve the instant coffee in the boiling water and place in a bowl with the cream and icing sugar. Whip until the cream is just holding its shape. Use half of the cream to sandwich the 3 cakes together. Spread the remaining cream over the top and sides of the cake. Lightly press the chocolate shavings into the cream around the edge of the cake.

5 Transfer to a serving plate. Lay the caraque over the top of the cake. Cut a few thin strips of baking paper and place on top of the caraque. Dust lightly with icing sugar, then carefully remove the paper. Serve.

dotty chocolate chip cake

serves 10
- 175 g/6 oz butter, softened, plus extra for greasing
- 175 g/6 oz caster sugar
- 3 eggs, beaten
- 175 g/6 oz plain flour
- 1 tsp baking powder
- 2 tbsp cocoa powder
- 55 g/2 oz white chocolate chips
- 40 g/1½ oz small coloured sweets, to decorate

icing
- 175 g/6 oz milk chocolate or plain chocolate
- 100 g/3½ oz unsalted butter or margarine
- 1 tbsp golden syrup

1 Preheat the oven to 160°C/325°F/Gas Mark 3. Grease and line the base of a 20-cm/8-inch round cake tin.

2 Place the butter, sugar, eggs, flour, baking powder and cocoa powder in a bowl and beat until just smooth. Stir in the chocolate chips, mixing evenly.

3 Spoon the mixture into the prepared tin. Bake in the preheated oven for 40–45 minutes, until risen and firm to the touch. Leave to cool in the tin for 5 minutes, then turn out and finish cooling on a wire rack.

4 To make the icing, place the chocolate, butter and golden syrup in a saucepan over a low heat and stir until just melted and smooth.

5 Remove from the heat and leave to cool until it begins to thicken enough to leave a trail when the spoon is lifted. Pour the icing over the top of the cake, allowing it to drizzle down the sides. Arrange the sweets over the top of the cake.

marble cake

serves 10
- 225 g/8 oz butter, softened, plus extra for greasing
- 55 g/2 oz plain chocolate, broken into pieces
- 1 tbsp strong black coffee
- 280 g/10 oz self-raising flour
- 1 tsp baking powder
- 225 g/8 oz caster sugar
- 4 eggs, beaten
- 50 g/1¾ oz ground almonds
- 2 tbsp milk
- 1 tsp vanilla essence

icing
- 125 g/4½ oz plain chocolate, broken into pieces
- 2 tbsp butter
- 2 tbsp water

1 Preheat the oven to 180°C/350°F/Gas Mark 4. Grease a 1.7-litre/3-pint ring mould. Put the chocolate and coffee in a heatproof bowl set over a saucepan of gently simmering water. Heat until melted. Leave to cool. Sift the flour and baking powder into a bowl. Add the butter, sugar, eggs, ground almonds and milk. Beat well until smooth.

2 Transfer one half of the mixture to another bowl and stir in the vanilla essence. Stir the cooled soft chocolate into the other half of the mixture. Place spoonfuls of the 2 mixtures alternately into the ring mould, then drag a skewer through to create a marbled effect. Smooth the top. Bake in the preheated oven for 50–60 minutes, until risen and a skewer inserted into the centre comes out clean. Leave to cool in the mould for 5 minutes, then turn out and finish cooling on a wire rack.

3 To make the icing, put the chocolate, butter and water into a heatproof bowl set over a saucepan of gently simmering water. Heat until melted and remove from the heat. Stir and pour over the cake, working quickly to coat the top and sides. Leave to set before serving.

gooey orange chocolate chip cake

serves 6
- 175 g/6 oz butter, softened, plus extra for greasing
- 2 oranges
- 175 g/6 oz plain white flour
- 2 tsp baking powder
- 175 g/6 oz golden caster sugar
- 3 eggs, beaten
- 1 tsp vanilla extract
- 100 g/3½ oz plain chocolate chips

sauce
- 85 g/3 oz plain chocolate, broken into pieces
- 40 g/1½ oz butter
- 3 tbsp orange juice

1 Preheat the oven to 180°C/350°F/Gas Mark 4. Grease and line a 23-cm/9-inch square cake tin.

2 Finely grate the rind from one of the oranges and reserve. Use a sharp knife to cut off all the peel and white pith from both oranges and carefully remove the segments, reserving any spare juices to add to the sauce. Chop half the segments into small pieces.

3 Sift the flour and baking powder into a large bowl and add the butter, sugar, eggs and vanilla extract. Beat well until the mixture is smooth, then stir in the orange rind and chopped orange.

4 Spoon the mixture into the prepared tin and smooth the surface with a palette knife. Sprinkle the chocolate chips over the top, spreading to the edges with a palette knife. Bake in the preheated oven for 35–40 minutes, or until well risen, golden brown and firm to the touch.

5 For the sauce, place the chocolate, butter and orange juice in a saucepan and heat gently, stirring, until melted and smooth. Serve the cake warm, topped with the reserved orange segments and with the sauce spooned over the top.

no-bake raisin biscuit cake

makes about 20 pieces

- 100 g/3½ oz butter
- 25 g/1 oz cocoa powder
- 200 g/7 oz digestive biscuits, crushed
- 85 g/3 oz dried cranberries or raisins
- 1 egg, beaten
- 125 g/4 oz milk chocolate, broken into squares

1 Grease and line a 450-g/1-lb loaf tin.

2 Place the butter and cocoa powder in a saucepan over a low heat until melted and the mixture is well combined. Remove from the heat and stir in the biscuits and dried fruit. Allow to cool for 5 minutes.

3 Add the egg and mix again until thoroughly mixed.

4 Spoon the mixture into the prepared loaf tin. Press down well using the back of the spoon.

5 Put the chocolate in a heatproof bowl set over a saucepan of gently simmering water. Heat until melted, then spread over the top of the cake. Leave to set for 1–2 hours in the refrigerator. Cut into squares and serve.

no-bake chocolate cake

serves 6–8

- 225 g/8 oz butter, plus extra for greasing
- 225 g/8 oz plain chocolate
- 3 tbsp black coffee
- 55 g/2 oz soft light brown sugar
- a few drops of vanilla extract
- 225 g/8 oz digestive biscuits, crushed
- 85 g/3 oz raisins
- 85 g/3 oz walnuts, chopped

1 Grease and line a 450-g/1-lb loaf tin.

2 Place the chocolate, butter, coffee, sugar and vanilla extract in a saucepan over a low heat and stir until the chocolate and butter have melted, the sugar has dissolved and the mixture is well combined.

3 Stir in the crushed biscuits, the raisins and walnuts. Spoon the mixture into the prepared loaf tin. Leave to set for 1–2 hours in the refrigerator, then turn out and cut into thin slices to serve.

Mmmm...
cookies, muffins & cupcakes

mega chip cookies

makes 12

- 225 g/8 oz butter, softened
- 140 g/5 oz caster sugar
- 1 egg yolk, beaten
- 2 tsp vanilla extract
- 225 g/8 oz plain flour
- 55 g/2 oz cocoa powder
- pinch of salt
- 85 g/3 oz milk chocolate chips
- 85 g/3 oz white chocolate chips
- 115 g/4 oz plain chocolate, roughly chopped

1 Preheat the oven to 190°C/375°F/Gas Mark 5. Line 2 baking trays with baking paper.

2 Put the butter and sugar into a bowl and mix well, then beat in the egg yolk and vanilla extract. Sift together the flour, cocoa powder and salt into the mixture, add both kinds of chocolate chips and stir until thoroughly combined.

3 Make 12 balls of the mixture, put them onto the prepared baking trays, spaced well apart, and flatten slightly. Press the pieces of plain chocolate into the cookies.

4 Bake in the preheated oven for 12–15 minutes. Leave to cool on the baking trays for 5–10 minutes, then transfer to wire racks to cool completely.

white chocolate cookies

makes 24

- 115 g/4 oz butter, softened
- 115 g/4 oz soft brown sugar
- 1 egg, beaten
- 250 g/9 oz self-raising flour
- pinch of salt
- 125 g/4½ oz white chocolate, chopped
- 50 g/1¾ oz Brazil nuts, chopped

1 Preheat the oven to 190°C/375°F/Gas Mark 5. Line 4 baking trays with baking paper.

2 Put the butter and sugar into a bowl and mix well, then beat in the egg. Sift the flour and salt into the mixture, add the chocolate chunks and nuts and stir until thoroughly combined.

3 Make 24 balls of the mixture, put them onto the prepared baking trays, spaced well apart, and flatten slightly.

4 Bake in the preheated oven for 10–12 minutes. Leave to cool on the baking trays for 5–10 minutes, then transfer to wire racks to cool completely.

chocolate orange cookies

makes about 30

- 90 g/3¼ oz butter, softened
- 60 g/2¼ oz caster sugar
- 1 egg
- 1 tbsp milk
- 280 g/10 oz plain flour, plus extra for dusting
- 2 tbsp cocoa powder

icing

- 175 g/6 oz icing sugar
- 3 tbsp orange juice
- a little plain chocolate, broken into pieces

1 Preheat the oven to 180°C/350°F/Gas Mark 4. Line 4 baking trays with baking paper.

2 Put the butter and sugar into a bowl and mix well, then beat in the egg and milk and stir until thoroughly combined. Sift the flour and cocoa powder into the bowl and gradually mix together to form a soft dough.

3 Roll out the dough on a lightly floured work surface until about 5 mm/¼ inch thick. Cut out rounds with a 5-cm/2-inch fluted round cutter and put them onto the baking trays, spaced well apart, and flatten slighty. Bake in the preheated oven for 10–12 minutes, or until golden brown. Leave to cool on the baking trays for a few minutes, then transfer the cookies to wire racks to cool completely.

4 To make the icing, sift the icing sugar in a bowl and stir in enough orange juice to form a thin icing that will coat the back of the spoon. Place a spoonful of icing in the centre of each biscuit and leave to set.

5 Place the plain chocolate in a heatproof bowl, set the bowl over a saucepan of gently simmering water and heat until melted. Drizzle thin lines of melted chocolate over the biscuits and leave to set before serving.

cappuccino cookies

makes about 30

- 225 g/8 oz butter, softened
- 140 g/5 oz caster sugar
- 1 egg yolk, beaten
- 2 sachets instant cappuccino powder mixed with 1 tbsp hot water
- 280 g/10 oz plain flour
- pinch of salt
- 175 g/6 oz white chocolate, broken into pieces
- cocoa powder, for dusting

1 Put the butter and sugar into a bowl and mix well with a wooden spoon, then beat in the egg yolk and cappuccino paste. Sift together the flour and salt into the mixture and stir until thoroughly combined. Halve the dough, wrap in clingfilm and chill in the refrigerator for 30–60 minutes.

2 Preheat the oven to 190°C/375°F/Gas Mark 5. Line 4 baking trays with baking paper.

3 Unwrap the dough and roll out between two sheets of baking paper. Stamp out cookies with a 6-cm/2½-inch round cutter and put them on the baking trays, spaced well apart, and flatten slighty.

4 Bake in the preheated oven for 10–12 minutes, until golden brown. Leave to cool for 5–10 minutes, then carefully transfer to wire racks to cool completely.

5 When the cookies are cool, place the wire racks over a sheet of baking paper. Put the chocolate into a heatproof bowl and melt over a pan of gently simmering water. Remove the bowl from the heat and leave to cool, then spoon the chocolate over the cookies. Gently tap the wire racks to level the surface and leave to set. Dust lightly with cocoa powder.

chocolate & coffee wholemeal cookies

makes 24

- 175 g/6 oz butter
- 200 g/7 oz soft light brown sugar
- 1 egg
- 70 g/2½ oz plain flour
- 1 tsp bicarbonate of soda
- pinch of salt
- 70 g/2½ oz wholemeal flour
- 1 tbsp bran
- 225 g/8 oz plain chocolate chips
- 185 g/6½ oz rolled oats
- 1 tbsp strong coffee
- 100 g/3½ oz hazelnuts, toasted and roughly chopped

1 Preheat the oven to 190°C/375°F/Gas Mark 5. Line 4 baking trays with baking paper.

2 Put the butter and sugar into a bowl and mix well, then beat in the egg. Sift together the plain flour, bicarbonate of soda and salt into another bowl, then add in the wholemeal flour and bran. Mix in the egg mixture, then stir in the chocolate chips, oats, coffee and hazelnuts and mix well.

3 Make 24 balls of the mixture, put them onto the prepared baking trays, spaced well apart, and flatten slightly. Bake in the preheated oven for 16–18 minutes, or until golden brown. Leave to cool for 5–10 minutes, then transfer to wire racks to cool completely.

chocolate sprinkle cookies

makes about 30

- 225 g/8 oz butter, softened
- 140 g/5 oz caster sugar
- 1 egg yolk, lightly beaten
- 2 tsp vanilla extract
- 225 g/8 oz plain flour, plus extra for dusting
- 55 g/2 oz cocoa powder
- pinch of salt
- 200 g/7 oz white chocolate, broken into pieces
- 85 g/3 oz chocolate sprinkles (vermicelli), to decorate

1 Put the butter and sugar into a bowl and mix well with a wooden spoon, then beat in the egg yolk and vanilla extract. Sift together the flour, cocoa powder and the salt into the mixture and stir until thoroughly combined. Halve the dough, wrap in clingfilm and chill in the refrigerator for 30–60 minutes.

2 Preheat the oven to 190°C/375°F/Gas Mark 5. Line 4 baking sheets with baking paper.

3 Unwrap the dough and roll out between 2 pieces of baking paper to about 5 mm/¼ inch thick and stamp out 30 cookies with a 6–7-cm/2½–2¾-inch fluted round cutter. Put them on the prepared baking trays, spaced well apart, and flatten slighty.

4 Bake in the preheated oven for 10–12 minutes. Leave to cool on the baking trays for 5–10 minutes, then transfer to wire racks to cool completely.

5 Put the pieces of white chocolate into a heatproof bowl and melt over a pan of gently simmering water, then immediately remove from the heat. Spread the melted chocolate over the cookies, leave to cool slightly and then sprinkle with the chocolate sprinkles. Leave to cool and set.

nutty drizzle cookies

makes 24

- 200 g/7 oz butter or margarine
- 275 g/9¾ oz brown sugar
- 1 egg
- 140 g/5 oz plain flour, sifted
- 1 tsp baking powder
- 1 tsp bicarbonate of soda
- 125 g/4½ oz rolled oats
- 1 tbsp bran
- 1 tbsp wheatgerm
- 115 g/4 oz mixed nuts, toasted and roughly chopped
- 200 g/7 oz plain chocolate chips
- 115 g/4 oz mixed raisins and sultanas
- 175 g/6 oz plain chocolate, roughly chopped

1 Preheat the oven to 180°C/350°F/Gas Mark 4. Line 4 baking trays with baking paper.

2 Put the butter and sugar into a bowl and mix well, then beat in the egg. Add the flour, baking powder, bicarbonate of soda, oats, bran and wheatgerm, and mix together until well combined. Finally, stir in the nuts, chocolate chips and dried fruit.

3 Make 24 balls of the mixture, put them onto the prepared baking trays, spaced well apart, and flatten slightly. Bake in the preheated oven for 12–15 minutes. Leave to cool on the baking trays for 5–10 minutes, then transfer to wire racks to cool completely.

4 Put the chocolate pieces in a heatproof bowl set over a saucepan of gently simmering water until melted. Stir the chocolate, then leave to cool slightly. Use a spoon to drizzle the chocolate over the biscuits, or spoon it into a piping bag and pipe zig-zag lines over the biscuits.

viennese fingers

makes about 16

- 100 g/3½ oz unsalted butter, plus extra for greasing
- 25 g/1 oz golden caster sugar
- ½ tsp vanilla extract
- 100 g/3½ oz self-raising flour
- 100 g/3½ oz plain chocolate, roughly chopped

1 Preheat the oven to 160°C/325°F/Gas Mark 3. Lightly grease 2 baking trays.

2 Place the butter, sugar and vanilla extract in a bowl and cream together until pale and fluffy. Stir in the flour, mixing evenly to a fairly stiff dough.

3 Place the mixture in a piping bag fitted with a large star nozzle and pipe about 16 fingers, each 6 cm/2½ inches long, onto the prepared baking trays.

4 Bake in the preheated oven for 10–15 minutes, until a pale golden colour. Cool for 2–3 minutes on the baking trays, then transfer to wire racks to cool completely.

5 Place the chocolate in a small heatproof bowl set over a pan of gently simmering water until melted. Remove from the heat. Dip the ends of each biscuit into the chocolate to coat, then place on a sheet of baking paper and leave to set.

chocolate chunk muffins

makes 12

- 280 g/10 oz plain white flour
- 1 tbsp baking powder
- pinch of salt
- 115 g/4 oz caster sugar
- 175 g/6 oz chocolate chunks
- 2 eggs, beaten
- 250 ml/9 fl oz milk
- 6 tbsp sunflower oil or 85 g/3 oz butter, melted and cooled
- 1 tsp vanilla extract

1 Preheat the oven to 200°C/400°F/Gas Mark 6. Line a 12-cup muffin tin with muffin paper cases. Sift the flour, baking powder and salt into a large bowl. Stir in the sugar and chocolate chunks.

2 Place the eggs, milk, oil and vanilla extract in a separate mixing bowl and mix well. Add the wet ingredients to the dry ingredients and stir gently until just combined.

3 Spoon the mixture into the paper cases and bake in the preheated oven for about 20 minutes, until well risen, golden brown and firm to the touch. Serve warm or cold.

triple chocolate muffins

makes 12

- 250 g/9 oz plain flour
- 25 g/1 oz cocoa powder
- 2 tsp baking powder
- ½ tsp bicarbonate of soda
- 100 g/3½ oz plain chocolate chips
- 100 g/3½ oz white chocolate chips
- 2 eggs, beaten
- 300 ml/10 fl oz soured cream
- 85 g/3 oz light muscovado sugar
- 85 g/3 oz butter, melted and cooled

1 Preheat the oven to 200°C/400°F/Gas Mark 6. Line a 12-cup muffin tin with muffin paper cases. Sift the flour, cocoa powder, baking powder and bicarbonate of soda into a large bowl, then stir in the plain and white chocolate chips.

2 Place the eggs, soured cream, sugar and butter in a separate mixing bowl and mix well. Add the wet ingredients to the dry ingredients and stir gently until just combined.

3 Spoon the mixture into the paper cases and bake in the preheated oven for 20 minutes, or until well risen and firm to the touch. Serve warm or cold.

chocolate orange muffins

makes 8–10
- 125 g/4½ oz self-raising flour
- 125 g/4½ oz self-raising wholemeal flour
- 25 g/1 oz ground almonds
- 55 g/2 oz soft brown sugar
- rind and juice of 1 orange
- 175 g/6 oz cream cheese
- 2 eggs
- 55 g/2 oz plain chocolate chips

1 Preheat the oven to 190°C/375°F/Gas Mark 5. Line a 10-cup muffin tin with muffin paper cases.

2 Sift the flours into a large bowl, then stir in the ground almonds and sugar.

3 Place the orange rind and juice, the cream cheese, the eggs and the chocolate chips in a separate mixing bowl and mix well. Add the wet ingredients to the dry ingredients and stir gently until just combined.

4 Spoon the mixture into the paper cases and bake in the preheated oven for 20–25 minutes, or until well risen and golden brown. Serve warm or cold.

spiced chocolate muffins

makes 12

- 250 g/9 oz plain flour
- 1 tsp bicarbonate soda
- 2 tbsp cocoa powder
- 1 tsp allspice
- 200 g/7 oz plain chocolate chips
- 100 g/3½ oz butter, softened
- 150 g /5½ oz caster sugar
- 115 g/4 oz brown sugar
- 2 eggs
- 150 ml/5 fl oz soured cream
- 5 tbsp milk

1 Preheat the oven to 190°C/375°F/Gas Mark 5. Line a 12-cup muffin tin with muffin paper cases. Sift the flour, bicarbonate of soda, cocoa powder and allspice into a large bowl, then stir in the chocolate chips.

2 Place the butter, caster sugar and brown sugar in a separate mixing bowl and mix well. Beat in the eggs, soured cream and milk until thoroughly mixed. Add the wet ingredients to the dry ingredients and stir gently until just combined.

3 Spoon the mixture into the paper cases and bake in the preheated oven for 25–30 minutes, or until well risen and firm to the touch. Serve warm or cold.

coffee & cream muffins

makes 12

- 280 g/10 oz plain white flour
- 1 tbsp baking powder
- pinch of salt
- 115 g/4 oz soft dark brown sugar
- 2 eggs, beaten
- 200 ml/7 fl oz double cream
- 6 tbsp sunflower oil or 85 g/3 oz butter, melted and cooled
- 2 tbsp instant coffee granules mixed with 2 tbsp boiling water
- 300 ml/10 fl oz whipping cream
- cocoa powder, for dusting
- 12 chocolate-covered coffee beans, to decorate

1 Preheat the oven to 200°C/400°F/Gas Mark 6. Line a 12-cup muffin tin with muffin paper cases. Sift the flour, baking powder and salt into a large bowl, then stir in the sugar.

2 Place the eggs, double cream, oil, and the cooled, dissolved coffee in a separate mixing bowl and mix well. Add the wet ingredients to the dry ingredients and stir gently until just combined.

3 Spoon the mixture into the paper cases and bake in the preheated oven for 20–25 minutes, or until golden brown and firm to the touch.

4 Leave the muffins in the tin for 5 minutes then transfer to a wire rack and leave to cool. Just before serving, whisk the whipping cream until it holds its shape. Spoon a dollop of the cream on top of each muffin, dust lightly with cocoa powder and top with a chocolate-covered coffee bean.

chocolate butterfly cupcakes

makes 12

- 125 g/4½ oz soft margarine
- 125 g/4½ oz caster sugar
- 150 g/5½ oz self-raising flour, sifted
- 2 eggs
- 2 tbsp cocoa powder
- 25 g/1 oz plain chocolate, melted

lemon buttercream

- 100 g/3½ oz butter, softened
- 225 g/8 oz icing sugar, sifted, plus extra for dusting
- grated rind of ½ lemon
- 1 tbsp lemon juice

1 Preheat the oven to 180°C/350°F/Gas Mark 4. Place 12 paper cases in a shallow bun tin. Place the margarine, caster sugar, flour, eggs and cocoa powder in a large bowl, and beat until the mixture is just smooth. Beat in the melted chocolate.

2 Spoon the mixture into the paper cases, filling them three-quarters full. Bake in the preheated oven for 15 minutes, or until well risen. Transfer to a wire rack and leave to cool completely.

3 For the buttercream, place the butter in a mixing bowl and beat until fluffy. Gradually add in the icing sugar, lemon rind and lemon juice, beating well with each addition.

4 Cut the top off each cake, using a serrated knife. Cut each cake top in half. Spread the lemon buttercream over the cut surface of each cake and push the two pieces of cake top into the icing to form wings. Dust with icing sugar.

dark & white fudge cupcakes

makes 20

- 200 ml/7 fl oz water
- 85 g/3 oz butter
- 85 g/3 oz caster sugar
- 1 tbsp golden syrup
- 3 tbsp milk
- 1 tsp vanilla essence
- 1 tsp bicarbonate of soda
- 225 g/8 oz plain flour
- 2 tbsp cocoa powder

icing

- 50 g/1¾ oz plain chocolate
- 4 tbsp water
- 50 g/1¾ oz butter
- 50 g/1¾ oz white chocolate
- 350 g/12 oz icing sugar

to decorate

- 100 g/3½ oz plain chocolate shavings
- 100 g/3½ oz white chocolate shavings

1 Preheat the oven to 180°C/350°F/Gas Mark 4. Place 20 paper cases in 2 shallow bun tins. Put the water, butter, sugar and syrup in a saucepan. Heat gently, stirring, until the sugar has dissolved, then bring to the boil. Reduce the heat and cook gently for 5 minutes. Remove from the heat and leave to cool.

2 Meanwhile, put the milk and vanilla essence in a bowl. Add the bicarbonate of soda and stir to dissolve. Sift the flour and cocoa powder into a separate bowl and add the syrup mixture. Stir in the milk and vanilla essence and beat until smooth. Spoon the mixture into the paper cases until they are two-thirds full.

3 Bake the cupcakes in the preheated oven for 20 minutes, or until well risen and firm to the touch. Transfer to wire racks and leave to cool.

4 To make the icing, break the plain chocolate into a small heatproof bowl, add half the water and half the butter, and set the bowl over a saucepan of gently simmering water until melted. Stir until smooth and leave to stand over the water. Repeat with the white chocolate and remaining water and butter. Sift half the icing sugar into each bowl and beat until smooth and thick. Top the cupcakes with the icing. Serve decorated with chocolate shavings.

mocha cupcakes with whipped cream

makes 20

- 2 tbsp instant espresso coffee powder
- 85 g/3 oz butter
- 85 g/3 oz caster sugar
- 1 tbsp clear honey
- 200 ml/7 fl oz water
- 225 g/8 oz plain flour
- 2 tbsp cocoa powder
- 1 tsp bicarbonate of soda
- 3 tbsp milk
- 1 large egg, beaten

topping

- 225 ml/8 fl oz whipping cream
- cocoa powder, for dusting

1 Preheat the oven to 180°C/350°F/Gas Mark 4. Place 20 paper cases in 2 shallow bun tins. Place the coffee powder, butter, sugar, honey and water in a saucepan and heat gently, stirring, until the sugar has dissolved. Bring to the boil, then reduce the heat and leave to simmer for 5 minutes. Pour into a large heatproof bowl and leave to cool.

2 When the mixture has cooled, sift in the flour and cocoa powder. Place the bicarbonate of soda and milk in a bowl and stir to dissolve, then add to the mixture with the egg and beat together until smooth. Spoon the mixture into the paper cases.

3 Bake in the preheated oven for 15–20 minutes, or until well risen and firm to the touch. Transfer to wire racks to cool completely.

4 For the topping, place the cream in a bowl and whip until it holds its shape. Spoon heaped teaspoonfuls of cream on top of each cake, then dust lightly with sifted cocoa powder.

rocky mountain cupcakes

makes 10

- 140 g/5 oz butter, softened
- 140 g/5 oz caster sugar
- 1 tsp vanilla extract
- 3 eggs, beaten
- 150 g/5½ oz self-raising flour
- 55 g/2 oz cocoa powder

topping

- 50 g/1¾ oz plain chocolate
- 2 tbsp water
- 25 g/1 oz butter
- 175 g/6 oz icing sugar
- 85 g/3 oz mini marshmallows
- 40 g/1½ oz walnuts, roughly chopped
- 55 g/2 oz milk chocolate, broken into pieces

1 Preheat the oven to 180°C/350°F/Gas Mark 4. Put 10 paper cases in a shallow bun tin. Place the butter and sugar in a large bowl and beat together until light and fluffy, then beat in the vanilla extract. Gradually beat in the eggs. Sift the flour and cocoa powder together and fold into the mixture. Spoon the mixture into the paper cases.

2 Bake in the preheated oven for 20–25 minutes, or until springy to the touch. Transfer to a wire rack to cool completely. To make the icing, break the chocolate into a small heatproof bowl, add the water and the butter, and set the bowl over a saucepan of gently simmering water until melted. Stir until smooth and leave to stand over the water. Sift the icing sugar into the bowl and beat until smooth and thick.

3 To decorate, pipe the icing on top of each cake to form a peak in the centre. Mix the marshmallows and walnuts together and divide among the cakes, then press down lightly. Place the chocolate in a heatproof bowl, set the bowl over a saucepan of gently simmering water and heat until melted. Drizzle over the tops of the cakes and leave to set.

hot pecan brownie cupcakes

makes 6

- 115 g/4 oz butter, plus extra for greasing
- 115 g/4 oz plain chocolate, broken into pieces
- 2 eggs
- 115 g/4 oz soft light brown sugar
- 3 tbsp maple syrup
- 115 g/4 oz plain flour, sifted
- 55 g/2 oz pecan nuts, chopped

1 Preheat the oven to 180°C/350°F/Gas Mark 4. Grease 6 x 150-ml/5-fl oz ovenproof teacups or dishes (such as ramekins) with butter.

2 Put the chocolate and butter into a heatproof bowl set over a saucepan of gently simmering water and leave until melted, stirring occasionally. Cool for 5 minutes.

3 Place the eggs, sugar and maple syrup in a large bowl and beat together until well blended. Beat in the chocolate mixture, and then fold in the flour and two-thirds of the pecan nuts. Pour the mixture into the cups and scatter over the rest of the nuts.

4 Put the cups on a baking sheet and bake in the preheated oven for 25–30 minutes, or until the cupcakes are risen and crisp on top, but still feel slightly wobbly if lightly pressed. Serve warm.

black forest cupcakes

makes 12

- 85 g/3 oz plain chocolate
- 1 tsp lemon juice
- 4 tbsp milk
- 150 g/5½ oz
  self-raising flour
- 1 tbsp cocoa powder,
  plus extra to dust
- ½ tsp bicarbonate of soda
- 2 eggs
- 55 g/2 oz butter, softened
- 115 g/4 oz soft light
  brown sugar
- 25 g/1 oz dried and
  sweetened sour cherries,
  chopped
- 2 tbsp cherry liqueur
  (optional)
- 150 ml/5 fl oz double cream,
  softly whipped
- 5 tbsp cherry conserve

1 Preheat the oven to 180°C/350°F/Gas Mark 4. Put 12 paper cases in a shallow bun tin.

2 Break the chocolate into a heatproof bowl and set the bowl over a saucepan of gently simmering water until melted. Add the lemon juice to the milk and leave for 10 minutes – the milk will curdle a little.

3 Sift the flour, cocoa powder and bicarbonate of soda into a large bowl. Add the eggs, butter, sugar and milk mixture and beat until smooth. Fold in the melted chocolate and cherries. Spoon the mixture into the paper cases.

4 Bake the cupcakes in the preheated oven for 20–25 minutes, until risen and firm to the touch. Transfer to a wire rack and leave to cool.

5 When the cupcakes are cold, use a serrated knife to cut a circle from the top of each cupcake. Sprinkle the cakes with a little cherry liqueur, if using. Spoon the whipped cream into the centres and top with a small spoonful of conserve. Gently replace the cupcake tops and dust lightly with cocoa powder. Store in the refrigerator until ready to serve.

pear & chocolate cupcakes

makes 12

- 115 g/4 oz butter, softened
- 115 g/4 oz light soft brown sugar
- 2 eggs
- 100 g/3½ oz self-raising flour
- ½ tsp baking powder
- 2 tbsp cocoa powder
- 4 canned pear halves, drained and sliced
- 2 tbsp runny honey, warmed

1 Preheat the oven to 190°C/375°F/Gas Mark 5. Put 12 paper cases in a shallow bun tin.

2 Place the butter, sugar, eggs, flour, baking powder and cocoa powder in a large bowl, and beat until the mixture is just smooth. Spoon the mixture into the paper cases and smooth the tops. Arrange 2 pear slices on top of each cupcake.

3 Bake the cupcakes in the preheated oven for 20 minutes or until risen and just firm to the touch. Transfer to a wire cooling rack. While the cupcakes are still warm, glaze with the honey. Leave to cool completely.

Mmmm...
hot desserts

double chocolate brownies

makes 9 large or 16 small

- 115 g/4 oz butter, plus extra for greasing
- 115 g/4 oz plain chocolate, broken into pieces
- 300 g/10½ oz golden caster sugar
- pinch of salt
- 1 tsp vanilla extract
- 2 large eggs
- 140 g/5 oz plain flour
- 2 tbsp cocoa powder
- 100 g/3½ oz white chocolate chips

fudge sauce

- 55 g/2 oz butter
- 225 g/8 oz golden caster sugar
- 150 ml/5 fl oz milk
- 250 ml/9 fl oz double cream
- 225 g/8 oz golden syrup
- 200 g/7 oz plain chocolate, broken into pieces

1 Preheat the oven to 180°C/350°F/Gas Mark 4. Grease and line the base of an 18-cm/7-inch square baking tin.

2 Place the butter and chocolate in a small heatproof bowl set over a saucepan of gently simmering water until melted. Stir until smooth. Leave to cool slightly. Stir in the sugar, salt and vanilla extract. Add the eggs, one at a time, and beat until well blended.

3 Sift the flour and cocoa powder into the mixture and beat until smooth. Stir in the chocolate chips, then pour the mixture into the tin. Bake in the preheated oven for 35–40 minutes, or until the top is evenly coloured and a skewer inserted into the centre comes out almost clean. Leave to cool slightly while preparing the sauce.

4 To make the sauce, place the butter, sugar, milk, cream and syrup in a small saucepan and heat gently until the sugar has dissolved. Bring to the boil and stir for 10 minutes, or until the mixture is caramel-coloured. Remove from the heat and add the chocolate. Stir until smooth. Cut the brownies into squares and serve immediately with the sauce.

mochachino brownies with white mocha sauce

makes 8–10

- 115 g/4 oz butter, plus extra for greasing
- 115 g/4 oz plain chocolate
- 2 tbsp strong black coffee
- 250 g/9 oz golden caster sugar
- ½ tsp ground cinnamon
- 3 eggs, beaten
- 85 g/3 oz plain flour
- 55 g/2 oz milk chocolate chips
- 55 g/2 oz toasted walnuts, skinned and chopped, plus extra to decorate

white mocha sauce

- 100 ml/3½ fl oz double cream
- 85 g/3 oz white chocolate
- 1 tbsp strong black coffee

1 Preheat the oven to 180°C/350°F/Gas Mark 4. Grease and line a 23-cm/9-inch square baking tin.

2 Place the butter, chocolate and coffee in a medium saucepan over a low heat and stir until just melted and smooth. Cool slightly.

3 Beat in the sugar, cinnamon and eggs, then beat in the flour, chocolate chips and walnuts. Pour into the prepared tin.

4 Bake in the preheated oven for 30–35 minutes, until just firm but still moist inside. Cool in the tin then cut into squares or bars.

5 Meanwhile, make the sauce by placing all the ingredients in a small pan over a low heat, stirring occasionally, until melted and smooth.

6 Place the brownies on individual plates and spoon the warm sauce on top. Decorate with chopped walnuts and serve.

mint julep brownie cakes

makes 6–8

- 175 g/6 oz butter, plus extra for greasing
- 125 g/4½ oz self-raising flour, plus extra for dusting
- 150 g/5½ oz plain chocolate
- 2 eggs
- 200 g/7 oz dark muscovado sugar
- 3 tbsp bourbon
- 1 tbsp chopped fresh mint
- mint sprigs, to decorate

sauce

- 115 g/4 oz plain chocolate
- 125 ml/4 fl oz single cream
- ¼ tsp peppermint extract

1 Preheat the oven to 180°C/350°F/Gas Mark 4. Grease and flour a 28 x 18-cm/11 x 7-inch rectangular baking tin.

2 Place the chocolate and butter in a pan over a very low heat and stir occasionally until melted. Remove from the heat.

3 Beat together the eggs, sugar, bourbon and chopped mint, then beat quickly into the chocolate mixture. Fold in the flour and mix evenly.

4 Pour the mixture into the prepared tin and smooth the surface. Bake in the preheated oven for 30–35 minutes, until just firm, but still slightly soft inside.

5 Allow to cool in the tin for 15 minutes, then remove from the tin and use a 7.5-cm/3-inch cutter to stamp out 6–8 rounds.

6 To make the sauce, place the chocolate, cream and peppermint extract in a small pan and heat gently, stirring, until melted and smooth.

7 To serve, place the brownie cakes on serving plates, drizzle with the warm chocolate sauce and decorate with sprigs of mint.

rich ginger brownies with port cream

makes 8

- 175 g/6 oz butter, plus extra for greasing
- 200 g/7 oz plain chocolate
- 200 g/7 oz granulated sugar
- 4 eggs, beaten
- 2 tsp vanilla extract
- 1 tbsp stem ginger syrup
- 100 g/3½ oz plain flour
- 55 g/2 oz preserved stem ginger in syrup, chopped
- 25 g/1 oz chopped crystallised ginger, to decorate

port cream

- 200 ml/7 fl oz ruby port
- 200 ml/7 fl oz double cream
- 1 tbsp icing sugar
- 1 tsp vanilla extract

1 Preheat the oven to 180°C/350°F/Gas Mark 4. Grease a 23-cm/9-inch square baking tin.

2 Place the chocolate and butter in a saucepan and heat gently, stirring, until melted. Remove from the heat and stir in the sugar.

3 Beat the eggs, vanilla extract and ginger syrup into the chocolate mixture. Stir in the flour and ginger and mix well.

4 Pour the mixture into the prepared tin and bake in the preheated oven for 30–35 minutes, until just firm to the touch.

5 Meanwhile, make the port cream. Place the port in a saucepan and simmer over a medium–high heat until reduced to about 4 tablespoons. Cool. Whip the cream until beginning to thicken, then beat in the sugar, reduced port and vanilla extract, continuing to whip until it holds soft peaks.

6 Remove the brownies from the oven, cool for 2–3 minutes in the tin, then cut into 8 triangles. Place on individual serving plates and add a spoonful of port cream to each. Top with pieces of crystallised ginger and serve warm.

blonde brownie hearts
with raspberry sauce

makes 8

- 115 g/4 oz butter, plus extra for greasing
- 115 g/4 oz white chocolate
- 2 eggs, beaten
- 150 g/5½ oz caster sugar
- seeds from 1 vanilla pod
- 140 g/5 oz plain flour, plus extra for dusting
- 8 small squares plain chocolate

raspberry sauce

- 250 g/9 oz raspberries, fresh or frozen, thawed
- 2 tbsp amaretto
- 1 tbsp icing sugar

1 Preheat the oven to 180°C/350°F/Gas Mark 4. Grease and lightly flour 8 individual heart-shaped baking tins, each 150 ml/5 fl oz capacity.

2 Place the chocolate and butter in a pan over a low heat and heat gently, stirring, until just melted. Remove from the heat.

3 Whisk together the eggs, sugar and vanilla seeds until smooth and thick. Fold in the flour lightly, then stir in the chocolate mixture and mix evenly.

4 Pour the batter mixture into the tins, adding a square of chocolate to the centre of each, without pressing down. Bake in the preheated oven for about 20–25 minutes, until just firm. Leave in the tins for 5 minutes.

5 To make the raspberry sauce, place half the raspberries, the amaretto and icing sugar in a food processor or blender and process until smooth. Transfer the mixture to a sieve placed on top of a bowl and rub through to remove the pips.

6 Run a knife around the edge of each heart to loosen from the tin and turn out onto individual plates. Spoon the raspberry sauce around the brownies and decorate with the remaining raspeberries.

chocolate blueberry tarts

makes 10

pastry

- 175 g/6 oz plain flour, plus extra for dusting
- 40 g/1½ oz cocoa powder
- 55 g/2 oz caster sugar
- pinch of salt
- 125 g/4½ oz butter
- 1 egg yolk
- 200 g/7 oz blueberries
- 2 tbsp cassis
- 10 g/¼ oz icing sugar, sifted

filling

- 140 g/5 oz plain chocolate, broken into pieces
- 225 ml/8 fl oz double cream
- 150 ml/5 fl oz soured cream

1 To make the pastry, put the flour, cocoa, sugar and salt in a food processor and pulse to mix. Add the butter, pulse again, then add the egg yolk and a little cold water to form a dough. If you do not have a processor, put the flour, cocoa, sugar and salt in a large bowl and rub in the butter until the mixture resembles breadcrumbs. Add the egg and a little cold water to form a dough. Cover the pastry with clingfilm and chill in the refrigerator for 30 minutes.

2 Preheat the oven to 180°C/350°F/Gas Mark 4. Remove the pastry from the refrigerator and roll out onto a lightly floured work surface. Use to line ten 10-cm/4-inch tart cases.

3 Put the blueberries, cassis and icing sugar in a saucepan and warm through so the berries become shiny, but do not burst. Remove from the heat and leave to cool.

4 For the filling, melt the chocolate in a heatproof bowl set over a saucepan of gently simmering water, then cool slightly. Whip the double cream until stiff and fold in the soured cream and chocolate.

5 Transfer the tart cases to a serving plate and divide the chocolate filling between them, smoothing the surface, then top with the blueberries.

hot chocolate soufflés with coffee sabayon

serves 6

- butter, for greasing
- 55 g/2 oz golden caster sugar, plus extra for coating
- 3 tbsp cornflour
- 250 ml/9 fl oz milk
- 115 g/4 oz plain chocolate, broken into pieces
- 4 eggs, separated
- icing sugar, for dusting

coffee sabayon

- 2 eggs
- 3 egg yolks
- 85 g/3 oz golden caster sugar
- 4 tsp instant coffee granules
- 2 tbsp brandy

1 Preheat the oven to 190°C/375°F/Gas Mark 5. Grease 6 medium-sized ramekins with butter and coat with caster sugar. To make the soufflés, place the cornflour in a bowl. Add a little milk and stir until smooth. Pour the remaining milk into a heavy-based saucepan and add the chocolate. Heat gently until the chocolate has melted, then stir. Pour the chocolate milk onto the cornflour paste, stirring. Return to the pan and bring to the boil, stirring. Simmer for 1 minute. Remove from the heat and stir in the egg yolks, one at a time. Cover and cool slightly.

2 Place the egg whites in a large, spotlessly clean, greasefree bowl and whisk until beginning to stand in soft peaks. Gradually whisk in the caster sugar until stiff but not dry. Stir a little of the meringue into the chocolate mixture, then carefully fold in the remainder. Pour into the prepared ramekins and bake in the preheated oven for 25–30 minutes, or until the soufflés are well risen and wobble slightly when pushed.

3 Just before the soufflés are ready, make the coffee sabayon. Place all the ingredients in a heavy-based saucepan. Place the saucepan over a very low heat and whisk constantly, until the mixture is thick and light. Dust a little icing sugar over the soufflés and serve immediately, with the sabayon.

individual chocolate fondant puddings

serves 4

- 100 g/3½ oz butter, plus extra for greasing
- 100 g/3½ oz golden caster sugar, plus extra for sprinkling
- 100 g/3½ oz plain chocolate, broken into pieces
- 2 eggs
- 1 tsp vanilla extract
- 2 tbsp plain flour
- icing sugar, sifted, for dusting
- lightly whipped cream, to serve

1 Preheat the oven to 200°C/400°F/Gas Mark 6. Grease 4 x 175-ml/6-fl oz pudding basins or ramekin dishes with butter and sprinkle with caster sugar.

2 Place the butter and chocolate in a heatproof bowl set over a saucepan of gently simmering water until melted. Stir until smooth. Leave to cool.

3 Place the eggs, vanilla extract, caster sugar and flour in a bowl and whisk together. Stir in the melted chocolate mixture. Pour into the prepared pudding basins and place on a baking tray. Bake in the preheated oven for 12–15 minutes, or until the puddings are well risen and set on the outside but still molten inside.

4 Leave to stand for 1 minute, then turn the puddings out onto serving plates. Dust with icing sugar and serve immediately with whipped cream.

chocolate orange pots

serves 4

- 1 orange
- 125 g/4½ oz plain chocolate, broken into pieces
- 30 g/1 oz butter
- 3 tbsp maple syrup
- 1 tbsp orange liqueur
- 125 g/4½ oz crème fraîche
- strips of orange zest, to decorate

1 Cut the white pith and peel from the orange and lift out the segments, catching the juices in a bowl. Cut the segments into small chunks.

2 Place the chocolate, butter, maple syrup and liqueur in a small pan with the reserved orange juices and heat very gently, stirring, until smooth.

3 Stir in 4 tablespoons of the crème fraîche and the orange chunks.

4 Spoon the mixture into serving dishes, then top each with a spoonful of the remaining crème fraîche.

5 Scatter strips of orange zest over the top and serve warm.

pear & hazelnut pancakes

serves 4

- 200 g/7 oz chocolate hazelnut spread
- 8 ready-made pancakes
- 4 ripe pears, peeled, cored and chopped
- 40 g/1½ oz butter, melted
- 2 tbsp demerara sugar
- 55 g/2 oz toasted chopped hazelnuts, to serve

1 Preheat the grill to high. Warm the chocolate spread gently in a small saucepan until softened.

2 Using a palette knife, spread each pancake with a little of the warmed chocolate spread.

3 Arrange the pears over the chocolate spread, then bring the opposite sides of the pancakes over the filling to enclose it.

4 Lightly brush an ovenproof dish with a little of the melted butter.

5 Arrange the pancakes in the dish. Brush the pancakes with the remaining melted butter and sprinkle with the demerara sugar.

6 Place the dish under the preheated grill and cook for 4–5 minutes, until bubbling and lightly browned.

7 Scatter the toasted hazelnuts over the pancakes and serve hot.

chocolate filo parcels

makes 18

- 55–85 g/2–3 oz butter, melted, plus extra for greasing
- 85 g/3 oz ground hazelnuts
- 1 tbsp finely chopped fresh mint
- 125 ml/4 fl oz soured cream
- 2 eating apples, peeled and grated
- 55 g/2 oz plain chocolate, melted
- 9 sheets filo pastry, about 15 cm/6 inches square
- icing sugar, sifted, for dusting

1 Preheat the oven to 190°C/375°F/Gas Mark 5. Grease a baking tray. Mix the nuts, mint and soured cream in a bowl. Add the apples, stir in the chocolate and mix well.

2 Cut each pastry sheet into 4 squares. Brush 1 square with butter, then place a second square on top and brush with butter.

3 Place a tablespoonful of the chocolate mixture in the centre, bring up the corners and twist together. Repeat until all of the pastry and filling has been used.

4 Place the parcels on the prepared baking tray and bake in the preheated oven for about 10 minutes, until crisp and golden. Remove from the oven and leave to cool slightly.

5 Dust with icing sugar and serve.

chocolate apple lattice tart

serves 6
pastry

- 200 g/7 oz plain flour, plus extra for dusting
- 2 tbsp cocoa powder
- 3 tbsp caster sugar
- 100 g/3½ oz butter, diced, plus extra for greasing
- 1–2 egg yolks, beaten

filling

- 225 g/8 oz double cream
- 2 eggs, beaten
- 1 tsp ground cinnamon
- 115 g/4 oz plain chocolate, grated
- 4 eating apples, peeled, sliced and brushed with lemon juice
- 3 tbsp demerara sugar

1 To make the pastry, sift the flour and cocoa powder into a bowl. Stir in the sugar, then add the butter and rub in with your fingertips until the mixture resembles fine breadcrumbs. Stir in enough egg yolk to form a dough. Form into a ball, wrap in foil and chill for 45 minutes.

2 Preheat the oven to 180°C/350°F/Gas Mark 4. Grease a 20-cm/8-inch loose-based round tart tin. Roll out the dough on a lightly floured work surface and use three quarters of it to line the tin.

3 For the filling, beat together the cream, the eggs (reserving a little for glazing), cinnamon and chocolate. Place the apples in a bowl, pour over the cream mixture and stir. Spoon the mixture into the tart tin, then sprinkle over the demerara sugar.

4 Roll out the remaining dough and cut into long strips, then arrange over the tart to form a lattice pattern. Brush the pastry strips with the reserved egg, then bake in the preheated oven for 40–45 minutes.

5 Remove from the oven and leave to cool to room temperature.

pear tart with chocolate sauce

serves 6
- 60 g/2¼ oz butter, plus extra for greasing
- 100 g/3½ oz plain flour
- 25 g/1 oz ground almonds
- about 3 tbsp water

filling
- 50 g/1¾ oz butter
- 50 g/1¾ oz caster sugar
- 2 eggs, beaten
- 100 g/3½ oz ground almonds
- 2 tbsp cocoa powder
- a few drops of almond extract
- 400 g/14 oz canned pear halves in natural juice, drained

chocolate sauce
- 4 tbsp caster sugar
- 3 tbsp golden syrup
- 100 ml/3½ fl oz water
- 175 g/6 oz plain chocolate, broken into pieces
- 25 g/1 oz butter

1 Preheat the oven to 200°C/400°F/Gas Mark 6. Lightly grease a 20-cm/8-inch round tart tin.

2 Sift the flour into a mixing bowl and stir in the ground almonds. Rub in the butter with your fingertips until the mixture resembles breadcrumbs. Add enough water to mix to a soft dough. Cover and chill in the freezer for 10 minutes, then roll out and use to line the prepared tin. Prick the base with a fork and chill again.

3 To make the filling, beat the butter and sugar until light and fluffy. Beat in the eggs, then fold in the ground almonds, cocoa powder and almond extract. Spread the chocolate mixture over the base of the pastry case. Thinly slice each pear widthways, flatten slightly, then arrange the pears on top of the chocolate mixture, pressing down lightly. Bake in the preheated oven for 30 minutes, or until the filling has risen. Cool slightly and transfer to a serving plate.

4 To make the chocolate sauce, place the sugar, golden syrup and water in a saucepan and heat gently, stirring until the sugar dissolves. Boil gently for 1 minute. Remove from the heat, add the chocolate and butter and stir until melted and well combined. Serve with the tart.

chocolate pecan pie

serves 6–8

pastry

- 175 g/6 oz plain flour, plus extra for dusting
- 100 g/3½ oz butter
- 1 tbsp golden caster sugar
- 1 egg yolk, beaten with 1 tbsp water

filling

- 55 g/2 oz butter
- 3 tbsp cocoa powder
- 225 ml/8 fl oz golden syrup
- 3 eggs
- 70 g/2½ oz soft dark brown sugar
- 175 g/6 oz pecan nuts

1 To make the pastry, sift the flour into a bowl. Rub in the butter with your fingertips until the mixture resembles breadcrumbs. Stir in the sugar, then add the beaten egg yolk. Knead lightly to form a firm dough. Cover and chill for 1½ hours.

2 Preheat the oven to 190°C/375°F/Gas Mark 5. On a lightly floured surface, roll out the pastry and use to line a 20-cm/8-inch round tart tin. Put a baking tray in the oven.

3 To make the filling, put the butter in a saucepan and heat gently until melted. Sift in the cocoa powder and add the golden syrup. Put the eggs and sugar in a bowl and beat together. Stir in the butter mixture and the pecan nuts.

4 Pour the mixture into the pastry case, place on the preheated baking tray and bake in the preheated oven for 35–40 minutes, until the filling is just set. Allow to cool slightly and serve warm.

chocolate meringue pie

serves 6

- 55 g/2 oz butter
- 225 g/8 oz plain chocolate digestive biscuits, crushed

filling

- 3 egg yolks
- 4 tbsp caster sugar
- 4 tbsp cornflour
- 600 ml/1 pint milk
- 100 g/3½ oz plain chocolate, broken into pieces

meringue

- 2 egg whites
- 100 g/3½ oz caster sugar
- ½ tsp vanilla extract

1 Preheat the oven to 190°C/375°F/Gas Mark 5. Melt the butter and stir in the biscuit crumbs until well combined. Press the mixture firmly into the base and up the sides of a 23-cm/9-inch round tart tin.

2 To make the filling, beat the egg yolks, sugar and cornflour in a large bowl until they form a smooth paste. Heat the milk in a heavy-based saucepan until almost boiling, then slowly pour it onto the egg mixture, whisking well.

3 Return the mixture to the saucepan and cook gently, whisking until it thickens. Remove from the heat. Melt the chocolate in a heatproof bowl set over a saucepan of gently simmering water. Whisk into the egg mixture and pour into the biscuit base.

4 To make the meringue, whisk the egg whites in a large mixing bowl until soft peaks form. Gradually whisk in about two thirds of the sugar until the mixture is stiff and glossy. Fold in the remaining sugar and the vanilla extract.

5 Spread the meringue over the chocolate filling, swirling the surface with the back of a spoon to give it an attractive finish. Bake in the centre of the preheated oven for 30 minutes, or until the meringue is golden. Serve the pie hot or just warm.

hot chocolate cheesecake

serves 8–10

pastry

- 55 g/2 oz butter, plus extra for greasing
- 150 g/5½ oz plain flour, plus extra for dusting
- 2 tbsp cocoa powder
- 2 tbsp golden caster sugar
- 25 g/1 oz ground almonds
- 1 egg yolk

filling

- 2 eggs, separated
- 75 g/2¾ oz golden caster sugar
- 350 g/12 oz cream cheese
- 4 tbsp ground almonds
- 150 ml/5 fl oz double cream
- 25 g/1 oz cocoa powder, sifted
- 1 tsp vanilla extract
- icing sugar, sifted, for dusting
- milk chocolate, grated, to decorate

1 Grease a 20-cm/8-inch loose-based round cake tin. To make the pastry, sift the flour and cocoa powder into a bowl and rub in the butter with your fingertips until the mixture resembles fine breadcrumbs. Stir in the sugar and ground almonds. Add the egg yolk and enough water to make a soft dough.

2 Roll out the pastry on a lightly floured work surface and use to line the prepared tin. Leave to chill for 30 minutes. Preheat the oven to 160°C/325°F/ Gas Mark 3.

3 To make the filling, put the egg yolks and sugar in a large bowl and whisk until thick and pale. Whisk in the cream cheese, ground almonds, cream, cocoa powder and vanilla extract until well combined.

4 Put the egg whites in a large bowl and whisk until stiff but not dry. Stir a little of the egg whites into the cheese mixture, then fold in the remainder. Pour into the pastry case.

5 Bake in the preheated oven for 1½ hours, until well risen and just firm to the touch. Carefully remove from the tin, dust with icing sugar and sprinkle with grated chocolate. Serve the cheesecake warm.

chocolate fruit crumble

serves 4
- butter, for greasing
- 400 g/14 oz canned apricots in natural juice
- 450 g/1 lb cooking apples, peeled and thickly sliced

crumble topping
- 100 g/3½ oz plain flour
- 85 g/3 oz butter
- 50 g/1¾ oz porridge oats
- 4 tbsp caster sugar
- 55 g/2 oz plain or milk chocolate chips
- single or double cream, to serve

1 Preheat the oven to 180°C/350°F/Gas Mark 4. Lightly grease an ovenproof dish.

2 Drain the apricots, reserving 4 tablespoons of the juice. Place the apples and apricots in the prepared ovenproof dish with the reserved apricot juice and toss to mix.

3 To make the crumble topping, sift the flour into a mixing bowl and rub in the butter with your fingertips until the mixture resembles fine breadcrumbs. Stir in the porridge oats, sugar and chocolate chips.

4 Sprinkle the crumble mixture over the apples and apricots and smooth the top lightly. Do not press the crumble into the fruit.

5 Bake in the preheated oven for 40–45 minutes, or until the topping is golden. Serve hot with cream.

profiteroles &
chocolate sauce

serves 4
choux pastry
- 70 g/2½ oz butter, plus extra for greasing
- 200 ml/7 fl oz water
- 100 g/3½ oz plain flour, sifted
- 3 eggs, beaten

cream filling
- 300 ml/10 fl oz double cream
- 3 tbsp caster sugar
- 1 tsp vanilla extract

chocolate sauce
- 125 g/4½ oz plain chocolate, broken into small pieces
- 35 g/1¼ oz butter
- 6 tbsp water
- 2 tbsp brandy

1 Preheat the oven to 200°C/400°F/Gas Mark 6. Grease a large baking tray.

2 To make the choux pastry, put the water and butter into a saucepan and bring to the boil. Immediately add all the flour, remove the pan from the heat and stir the mixture into a paste that leaves the sides of the pan clean. Leave to cool slightly. Beat in enough of the eggs to give the mixture a soft dropping consistency.

3 Transfer to a piping bag fitted with a 1-cm/½-inch plain nozzle. Pipe small balls onto the prepared baking tray. Bake in the preheated oven for 25 minutes. Remove from the oven. Pierce each ball with a skewer to allow the steam to escape.

4 To make the filling, whip together the cream, sugar and vanilla extract. Cut the pastry balls almost in half, then fill with cream.

5 To make the sauce, gently melt the chocolate and butter with the water in a heatproof bowl set over a saucepan of gently simmering water, stirring until smooth. Stir in the brandy. Pile the profiteroles into individual serving dishes or into a pyramid on a raised cake stand. Drizzle the sauce over the profiteroles and serve warm.

chocolate fondue

serves 6
- 1 pineapple
- 1 mango
- 12 physalis
- 250 g/9 oz fresh strawberries
- 250 g/9 oz seedless green grapes

fondue
- 250 g/9 oz plain chocolate, broken into pieces
- 150 ml/5 fl oz double cream
- 2 tbsp brandy

1 Using a sharp knife, peel and core the pineapple, then cut the flesh into cubes. Peel the mango and cut the flesh into cubes. Peel back the papery outer skin of the physalis and twist at the top to make a 'handle'. Arrange all the fruit on 6 serving plates and leave to chill in the refrigerator.

2 To make the fondue, place the chocolate and cream in a fondue pot. Heat gently, stirring constantly, until the chocolate has melted. Stir in the brandy until thoroughly blended and the chocolate mixture is smooth.

3 Place the fondue pot over the burner to keep warm. To serve, allow each guest to dip the fruit into the sauce, using fondue forks or bamboo skewers.

chocolate zabaglione

serves 4

- 4 egg yolks
- 4 tbsp caster sugar
- 50 g/1¾ oz plain chocolate
- 125 ml/4 fl oz Marsala wine
- cocoa powder, for dusting

1 Place the egg yolks and caster sugar in a large heatproof bowl and beat together using an electric whisk until the mixture is very pale.

2 Grate the chocolate finely and fold into the egg mixture. Fold in the Marsala wine.

3 Place the bowl over a saucepan of gently simmering water and set the electric whisk on the lowest speed or swap to a balloon whisk. Cook gently, whisking constantly, until the mixture thickens. Do not overcook or the mixture will curdle.

4 Spoon the hot mixture into 4 heatproof glasses and dust with cocoa powder. Serve warm.

Mmmm...
cool desserts

rich chocolate mousses

makes 4

- 300 g/10½ oz plain chocolate
- 5 tbsp caster sugar
- 1½ tbsp butter
- 1 tbsp brandy
- 4 eggs, separated
- cocoa powder, for dusting

1 Break the chocolate into small pieces and put it in a heatproof bowl over a saucepan of gently simmering water. Add the caster sugar and butter and melt together, stirring, until smooth. Remove from the heat, stir in the brandy, and leave to cool a little. Add the egg yolks and beat until smooth.

2 In a separate bowl, whisk the egg whites until stiff peaks form, then fold them into the chocolate mixture. Place a stainless steel cooking ring on each of 4 small serving plates, then spoon the mixture into each ring and smooth the surfaces. Transfer to the refrigerator and chill for at least 4 hours until set.

3 Remove the mousses from the refrigerator and carefully remove the cooking rings. Dust with cocoa powder and serve immediately.

brown sugar mocha cream dessert

serves 4

- 300 ml/10 fl oz double cream
- 1 tsp vanilla extract
- 85 g/3 oz fresh wholemeal breadcrumbs
- 85 g/3 oz dark brown sugar
- 1 tbsp instant coffee granules
- 2 tbsp cocoa powder
- milk chocolate, grated, to decorate

1 Whip together the cream and vanilla extract in a large bowl until thick and holding soft peaks.

2 Mix together the breadcrumbs, sugar, coffee and cocoa powder in a separate large bowl.

3 Layer the breadcrumb mixture with the whipped cream in serving glasses, finishing with a layer of whipped cream. Sprinkle with the grated chocolate.

4 Cover with clingfilm and chill in the refrigerator for several hours, or overnight.

5 Remove from the refrigerator and serve.

white chocolate tiramisù

serves 4

- 16 Italian sponge fingers
- 250 ml/9 fl oz strong black coffee, cooled to room temperature
- 4 tbsp almond-flavoured liqueur, such as amaretto
- 250 g/9 oz mascarpone cheese
- 300 ml/10 fl oz double cream
- 3 tbsp caster sugar
- 125 g/4½ oz white chocolate, grated
- 4 tbsp toasted flaked almonds, to decorate

1 Break the sponge fingers into pieces and divide half of them equally between 4 serving glasses. Mix together the coffee and liqueur in a jug, then pour half over the sponge fingers in the glasses.

2 Beat the mascarpone, cream, sugar and 50 g/1¾ oz of the chocolate in a bowl. Spread half the mixture over the coffee-soaked sponge fingers, then arrange the remaining sponge fingers on top. Pour over the remaining coffee mixture, then spread over the remaining cream mixture. Sprinkle with the remaining chocolate.

3 Cover with clingfilm and chill for at least 2 hours, or until required. Sprinkle over the flaked almonds before serving.

chocolate ice cream bites

serves 6
- 600 g/1 lb 5 oz good-quality ice cream
- 200 g/7 oz dark chocolate
- 2 tbsp butter

1 Line a baking tray with clingfilm.

2 Cut the ice cream into bite-sized cubes. Alternatively, using a melon baller, scoop out balls of ice cream and place them on the prepared baking tray. Stick a cocktail stick in each piece and return to the freezer until very hard.

3 Place the chocolate and the butter in a heatproof bowl set over a saucepan of gently simmering water until melted. Quickly dip the frozen ice cream cubes into the warm chocolate and return to the freezer. Keep them there until ready to serve.

chocolate banana sundae

serves 4
chocolate sauce
- 55 g/2 oz plain chocolate
- 4 tbsp golden syrup
- 15 g/½ oz butter
- 1 tbsp brandy or dark rum (optional)

sundae
- 150 ml/5 fl oz double cream
- 4 bananas, peeled
- 8 scoops good-quality vanilla ice cream
- 75 g/2¾ oz chopped mixed nuts, toasted
- milk or plain chocolate, grated
- 4 fan wafers, to serve

1 To make the chocolate sauce, break the chocolate into small pieces and place in a heatproof bowl with the golden syrup and butter. Set over a saucepan of gently simmering water until melted, stirring until well combined. Remove the bowl from the heat and stir in the brandy, if using.

2 Whip the cream until just holding its shape and slice the bananas. Place a scoop of ice cream in the bottom of each of 4 sundae glasses. Top with slices of banana, some chocolate sauce, a spoonful of cream and a generous sprinkling of nuts.

3 Repeat the layers, finishing with a good dollop of cream, then sprinkle with the remaining nuts and the grated chocolate. Serve with fan wafers.

chocolate hazelnut pots

serves 4
- 2 eggs
- 2 egg yolks
- 1 tbsp caster sugar
- 1 tsp cornflour
- 600 ml/1 pint milk
- 85 g/3 oz plain chocolate
- 4 tbsp chocolate hazelnut spread
- lightly whipped cream and chocolate caraque, to decorate

1 Preheat the oven to 160°C/325°F/Gas Mark 3.

2 Beat together the eggs, egg yolks, caster sugar and cornflour until well combined. Heat the milk in a small saucepan until it is almost boiling. Gradually pour the milk onto the eggs, whisking as you do so. Melt the chocolate and chocolate hazelnut spread in a heatproof bowl set over a saucepan of gently simmering water, then whisk the melted chocolate mixture into the egg mixture.

3 Pour into 4 small ovenproof dishes and cover the dishes with foil. Place them in a roasting tin. Fill the tin with boiling water until it comes halfway up the sides of the dishes. Bake in the preheated oven for 35–40 minutes, until the custard is just set.

4 Remove from the roasting tin and leave to cool, then chill until required. Serve decorated with whipped cream and chocolate caraque.

chocolate rum pots

makes 6

- 225 g/8 oz plain chocolate
- 4 eggs, separated
- 6 tbsp caster sugar
- 4 tbsp dark rum
- 4 tbsp double cream
- whipped cream and marbled chocolate shapes, to decorate

1 Put the chocolate in a heatproof bowl set over a saucepan of gently simmering water until melted. Leave to cool slightly.

2 Whisk the egg yolks with the caster sugar in a clean bowl until very pale and fluffy.

3 Drizzle the melted chocolate into the mixture and fold in together with the rum and double cream.

4 Whisk the egg whites in a greasefree bowl until soft peaks form. Fold the egg whites into the chocolate mixture in 2 batches. Divide the mixture among 6 serving dishes and chill in the refrigerator for at least 2 hours.

5 To serve, decorate with a little whipped cream and top with marbled chocolate shapes.

chocolate & vanilla creams

makes 4

- 450 ml/16 fl oz double cream
- 6 tbsp caster sugar
- 1 vanilla pod
- 200 ml/7 fl oz crème fraîche
- 2 tsp powdered gelatine
- 3 tbsp water
- 50 g/1¾ oz plain chocolate, broken into pieces
- marbled chocolate caraque, chopped, to decorate

1 Place the cream and sugar in a saucepan and add the vanilla pod. Heat gently, stirring until the sugar has dissolved, then bring to the boil. Reduce the heat and simmer for 2–3 minutes.

2 Remove the saucepan from the heat and take out the vanilla pod. Stir in the crème fraîche.

3 Sprinkle the gelatine over the water in a small heatproof bowl and let it go spongy, then set over a saucepan of hot water and stir until dissolved. Stir into the cream mixture. Pour half of this mixture into another mixing bowl.

4 Put the plain chocolate in a heatproof bowl set over a saucepan of simmering water until melted. Stir the melted chocolate into one half of the cream mixture. Pour the chocolate mixture into 4 individual glasses or glass serving dishes and chill for 15–20 minutes, until just set. While the chocolate mixture is chilling, keep the vanilla mixture at room temperature.

5 Spoon the vanilla mixture on top of the chocolate mixture and chill until the vanilla cream is set. When ready to serve, decorate with the chopped caraque.

chocolate meringues

makes 8
- 4 egg whites
- 200 g/7 oz caster sugar
- 1 tsp cornflour
- 40 g/1½ oz plain chocolate, grated

filling
- 100 g/3½ oz plain chocolate
- 150 ml/5 fl oz double cream
- 1 tbsp icing sugar
- 1 tbsp brandy (optional)

1 Preheat the oven to 140°C/275°F/Gas Mark 1. Line 2 baking trays with baking paper.

2 Whisk the egg whites until soft peaks form, then gradually whisk in half the caster sugar. Continue whisking until the mixture is very stiff and glossy.

3 Carefully fold in the remaining caster sugar, cornflour and grated chocolate with a metal spoon or palette knife. Spoon the mixture into a piping bag fitted with a large star or plain nozzle. Pipe 16 large rosettes or mounds onto the prepared baking trays.

4 Bake in the preheated oven for about 1 hour, changing the position of the baking trays after 30 minutes. Without opening the oven door, turn off the oven and leave the meringues to cool in the oven. Once cold, carefully peel off the baking paper.

5 To make the filling, melt the plain chocolate in a heatproof bowl set over a saucepan of gently simmering water and carefully spread it over the bases of the meringues. Stand them upside down on a wire rack until the chocolate has set. Whip the cream, icing sugar and brandy, if using, until the cream holds its shape, then use to sandwich the chocolate-coated meringues together in pairs.

chocolate trifle

serves 8

- 280 g/10 oz ready-made chocolate loaf cake
- 3–4 tbsp seedless raspberry jam
- 4 tbsp amaretto
- 250 g/9 oz frozen mixed berries, thawed
- chocolate truffles and chocolate shapes, to decorate

chocolate custard

- 6 egg yolks
- 55 g/2 oz caster sugar
- 1 tbsp cornflour
- 500 ml/18 fl oz milk
- 55 g/2 oz plain chocolate, broken into pieces

topping

- 225 ml/8 fl oz double cream
- 1 tbsp caster sugar
- ½ tsp vanilla extract

1 Cut the cake into slices and make 'sandwiches' with the raspberry jam. Cut the 'sandwiches' into cubes and place in a large glass serving bowl. Sprinkle with amaretto. Spread the berries over the cake.

2 To make the custard, put the egg yolks and sugar in a bowl and whisk until thick and pale. Stir in the cornflour. Put the milk in a saucepan and heat until almost boiling. Pour onto the yolk mixture, stirring. Return the mixture to the saucepan and bring just to the boil, stirring constantly until it thickens. Remove from the heat and leave to cool slightly. Put the chocolate in a heatproof bowl set over a saucepan of gently simmering water until melted, then add to the custard. Pour over the cake and berries. Cool, cover and chill for 2 hours, or until set.

3 To make the topping, put the cream in a bowl and whip until soft peaks form. Beat in the sugar and vanilla extract. Spoon over the trifle. Decorate with chocolate truffles and chocolate shapes and then chill until ready to serve.

white truffle cake

serves 12

- butter, for greasing
- 50 g/1¾ oz white chocolate
- 2 eggs
- 50 g/1¾ oz caster sugar
- 70 g/2½ oz plain flour

truffle topping

- 300 ml/10 fl oz double cream
- 350 g/12 oz white chocolate, broken into pieces
- 250 g/9 oz mascarpone cheese
- 50 g/1¾ oz white chocolate shavings

1 Preheat the oven to 180°C/ 350°F/Gas Mark 4. Grease and line the base of a 20-cm/8-inch round springform cake tin.

2 Melt the chocolate in a heatproof bowl set over a saucepan of gently simmering water.

3 Using a electric hand-held whisk, beat the eggs and sugar together in a large bowl until thick and pale – the mixture should leave a trail when the whisk is lifted. Sift the flour and gently fold into the egg mixture with a metal spoon. Add the melted chocolate.

4 Pour the mixture into the prepared tin and bake in the preheated oven for 25 minutes, or until springy to the touch. Leave to cool slightly in the tin, then transfer to a wire rack and leave to cool completely. Return the cold cake to the tin.

5 To make the topping, put the cream in a saucepan and bring to the boil, stirring constantly. Leave to cool slightly, then add the chocolate and stir until melted and combined. Remove from the heat and set aside until almost cool, stirring, then mix in the mascarpone cheese.

6 Pour on top of the cake. Chill in the refrigerator for 2 hours. Decorate with the chocolate shavings before serving.

citrus cake

serves 12

- 175 g/6 oz butter, plus extra for greasing
- 175 g/6 oz caster sugar
- 4 eggs, beaten
- 200 g/7 oz self-raising flour
- 1 tbsp cocoa powder
- 50 g/1¾ oz orange-flavoured plain chocolate, melted
- peeled orange segments, to decorate

orange mousse

- 2 eggs, separated
- 50 g/1¾ oz caster sugar
- 200 ml/7 fl oz freshly squeezed orange juice
- 2 tsp gelatine
- 3 tbsp water
- 300 ml/10 fl oz double cream

1 Preheat the oven to 180°C/350°F/Gas Mark 4. Grease a 20-cm/8-inch round springform cake tin and line the base with baking paper. Beat the butter and sugar in a bowl until light and fluffy. Gradually add the eggs, beating well after each addition. Sift together the flour and cocoa powder and fold into the creamed mixture. Fold in the melted chocolate.

2 Pour into the prepared tin and level the top. Bake in the preheated oven for 40 minutes, or until springy to the touch. Leave to cool for 5 minutes in the tin, then turn out onto a wire rack and leave to cool completely. Cut the cold cake horizontally into 2 layers.

3 To make the orange mousse, beat the egg yolks and sugar until pale, then whisk in the orange juice. Sprinkle the gelatine over the water in a small heatproof bowl and allow to go spongy, then place over a saucepan of hot water and stir until dissolved. Stir into the egg yolk mixture. Whip the cream until holding its shape, reserve a little for decoration, then fold the remainder into the orange mixture. Whisk the egg whites until standing in soft peaks, then fold in. Leave in a cool place until starting to set, stirring occasionally.

4 Place half of the cake back in the tin. Pour in the mousse and press the second cake layer on top. Chill until set. Transfer to a serving plate, spoon teaspoonfuls of cream around the top and decorate the centre with orange segments.

crispy chocolate pie

serves 6

- butter, for greasing
- 2 egg whites
- 100 g/3½ oz ground almonds
- 4 tbsp ground rice
- 125 g/4½ oz caster sugar
- ¼ tsp almond essence
- 225 g/8 oz plain chocolate, broken into small pieces
- 4 egg yolks
- 4 tbsp icing sugar
- 4 tbsp whisky
- 4 tbsp double cream

to decorate

- 150 ml/5 fl oz whipped cream
- marbled chocolate caraque

1 Preheat the oven to 160°C/325°F/Gas Mark 3. Grease a 20-cm/8-inch flan tin and line the base with baking paper. Whisk the egg whites until stiff peaks form. Gently fold in the ground almonds, ground rice, caster sugar and almond essence. Spread the mixture over the base and sides of the prepared tin. Bake in the preheated oven for 15 minutes.

2 Meanwhile, put the chocolate in a heatproof bowl set over a saucepan of gently simmering water until melted. Remove from the heat and cool slightly, then beat in the egg yolks, icing sugar, whisky and the double cream until thoroughly incorporated.

3 Remove the flan tin from the oven and pour in the chocolate mixture. Cover with foil, return to the oven and bake at the same temperature for 20–25 minutes, until set. Remove from the oven and leave to cool completely.

4 Cut the pie into 6 slices. Decorate each slice with whipped cream and the marbled chocolate caraque. Serve immediately.

mississippi mud pie

serves 8

pastry

- 225 g/8 oz plain flour, plus extra for dusting
- 2 tbsp cocoa powder
- 140 g/5 oz butter
- 2 tbsp caster sugar
- 1–2 tbsp cold water

filling

- 175 g/6 oz butter
- 350 g/12 oz soft dark brown sugar
- 4 eggs, lightly beaten
- 4 tbsp cocoa powder, sifted
- 150 g/5½ oz plain chocolate, broken into pieces
- 300 ml/10 fl oz single cream
- 1 tsp chocolate essence

to decorate

- 425 ml/15 fl oz double cream, whipped
- milk chocolate flakes

1 To make the pastry, sift the flour and cocoa powder into a mixing bowl. Rub in the butter with your fingertips until the mixture resembles fine breadcrumbs. Stir in the sugar and enough cold water to mix to a soft dough. Wrap the dough in clingfilm and chill in the refrigerator for 15 minutes.

2 Preheat the oven to 190°C/375°F/Gas Mark 5. Roll out the pastry on a lightly floured work surface and use to line a 23-cm/9-inch loose-based flan tin or ceramic flan dish. Line with baking paper and fill with baking beans. Bake in the preheated oven for 15 minutes. Remove the paper and beans from the pastry case and cook for a further 10 minutes until crisp.

3 To make the filling, beat the butter and sugar together in a bowl and gradually beat in the eggs with the cocoa powder. Melt the chocolate and beat it into the mixture with the single cream and the chocolate essence.

4 Reduce the oven temperature to 160°C/325°F/Gas Mark 3. Pour the mixture into the pastry case and bake for 45 minutes, or until the filling has set gently.

5 Let the mud pie cool completely, then transfer the pie to a serving plate. Cover with the whipped cream. Decorate the pie with chocolate flakes and then chill until ready to serve.

blackberry flan

serves 6

pastry
- 140 g/5 oz plain flour, plus extra for dusting
- 25 g/1 oz cocoa powder
- 55 g/2 oz icing sugar
- pinch of salt
- 85 g/3 oz butter, cut into small pieces
- ½ egg yolk

filling
- 300 ml/10 fl oz double cream
- 175 g/6 oz blackberry jam
- 225 g/8 oz plain chocolate, broken into pieces
- 25 g/1 oz butter, cut into small pieces

sauce
- 675 g/1 lb 8 oz blackberries, plus extra to decorate
- 1 tbsp lemon juice
- 2 tbsp caster sugar
- 2 tbsp crème de cassis

1 To make the pastry, sift the flour, cocoa powder, icing sugar and salt into a mixing bowl and make a well in the centre. Put the butter and egg yolk in the well and gradually mix in the dry ingredients. Knead lightly and form into a ball. Wrap the dough in clingfilm and chill in the refrigerator for 1 hour.

2 Preheat the oven to 180°C/350°F/Gas Mark 4. Roll out the pastry on a lightly floured work surface. Use it to line a 30 x 10-cm/12 x 4-inch rectangular flan tin and prick the pastry case with a fork. Line the base with baking paper and fill with baking beans. Bake in the preheated oven for 15 minutes. Take out of the oven and remove the paper and beans. Set aside to cool.

3 To make the filling, put the cream and jam in a saucepan and bring to the boil over a low heat. Remove the saucepan from the heat and stir in the chocolate and then the butter until melted and smooth. Pour the mixture into the pastry case and set aside to cool.

4 To make the sauce, put the blackberries, lemon juice and caster sugar in a food processor and process until smooth. Strain through a nylon sieve into a bowl and stir in the cassis. Set aside.

5 Remove the flan from the tin and place on a serving plate. Arrange the remaining blackberries on top and brush with a little of the blackberry and liqueur sauce. Serve the flan with the remaining sauce on the side.

chocolate & raspberry pavlova

serves 6
meringue
- 4 egg whites
- 225 g/8 oz caster sugar
- 1 tsp cornflour
- 1 tsp white wine vinegar
- 1 tsp vanilla extract

topping
- 300 ml/10 fl oz double cream
- 1 tbsp caster sugar
- 2 tbsp framboise liqueur
- 175 g/6 oz fresh raspberries
- 55 g/2 oz plain chocolate shavings

1 Preheat the oven to 150°C/300°F/Gas Mark 2.

2 In a large mixing bowl, whisk the egg whites until stiff and gradually whisk in 115 g/4 oz of the sugar. In a separate bowl, mix the remaining sugar with the cornflour and then whisk it into the egg white mixture; it should be very shiny and firm. Quickly fold the vinegar and vanilla extract into the egg white mixture.

3 Draw a 25-cm/10-inch circle on a sheet of baking paper, turn the paper over and place it on a baking tray. Pile the meringue onto the baking paper and spread evenly to the edge of the circle; swirl it around on top to make an attractive shape. Bake in the centre of the preheated oven for 1 hour.

4 Remove from the oven, leave to cool slightly, then peel off the paper. Place the meringue on a large serving plate. It will shrink and crack but do not worry about this.

5 One hour before serving, whip together the cream, sugar and liqueur until thick and floppy. Pile on top of the meringue and decorate with the raspberries and chocolate shavings. Chill before serving.

chocolate mousse tart

serves 8
- 85 g/3 oz digestive biscuits, crushed
- 85 g/3 oz amaretti biscuits, crushed
- 70 g/2½ oz butter, melted

topping
- 200 g/7 oz plain chocolate, broken into pieces
- 115 g/4 oz milk chocolate, broken into pieces
- 3 eggs, separated
- 55 g/2 oz caster sugar
- chocolate flakes, to decorate

1 To make the base, mix the digestive biscuits and amaretti biscuits with the butter and press well into the base of a 23-cm/9-inch springform cake tin. Chill in the refrigerator.

2 Melt the plain and milk chocolate in a heatproof bowl set over a saucepan of gently simmering water. Cool slightly, then add the egg yolks and mix well.

3 Whisk the egg whites until they form soft peaks, then add the caster sugar and whisk until stiff.

4 Fold the chocolate into the egg whites and pour over the biscuit base. Chill in the refrigerator for 8 hours, or overnight.

5 When you are ready to serve the tart, unmould it, transfer to a serving dish and crumble the chocolate flakes over the top.

brownie bottom cheesecake

serves 12

- 115 g/4 oz butter, plus extra for greasing
- 115 g/4 oz plain flour, plus extra for dusting
- 115 g/4 oz plain chocolate
- 200 g/7 oz caster sugar
- 2 eggs, beaten
- 50 ml /2 fl oz milk

topping

- 500 g/1 lb 2 oz soft cheese
- 125 g/4½ oz caster sugar
- 3 eggs, beaten
- 1 tsp vanilla essence
- 125 ml/4 fl oz natural yogurt
- plain chocolate, melted, to drizzle

1 Preheat the oven to 180°C/350°F/Gas Mark 4. Lightly grease and flour a 23-cm/9-inch square baking tin.

2 Melt the butter and chocolate in a saucepan over a low heat, stirring often, until smooth. Remove from the heat and beat in the sugar.

3 Add the eggs and milk, beating well. Stir in the flour, mixing just until blended. Spoon into the prepared tin, spreading evenly.

4 Bake in the preheated oven for 25 minutes. Remove from the oven while preparing the topping. Reduce the oven temperature to 160°C/325°F/Gas Mark 3.

5 To make the topping, beat together the cheese, sugar, eggs and vanilla essence until well blended. Stir in the yogurt, then pour over the brownie base. Bake for a further 45–55 minutes or until the centre is almost set.

6 Run a knife around the edge of the cake to loosen from the tin. Leave to cool before removing from the tin. Chill in the refrigerator for 4 hours or overnight before cutting into slices. Serve drizzled with melted chocolate.

deep chocolate cheesecake

serves 6–8
base
- 115 g/4 oz digestive biscuits, crushed
- 2 tsp cocoa powder
- 55 g/2 oz butter, melted, plus extra for greasing

chocolate layer
- 800 g/1 lb 12 oz mascarpone cheese
- 200 g/7 oz icing sugar, sifted
- juice of ½ orange
- finely grated rind of 1 orange
- 175 g/6 oz plain chocolate, melted
- 2 tbsp brandy
- plain chocolate leaves, to decorate

1 Grease a 20-cm/8-inch loose-based round cake tin.

2 To make the base, put the crushed biscuits, cocoa powder and melted butter into a large bowl and mix well. Press the biscuit mixture evenly over the base of the prepared tin.

3 Put the mascarpone cheese and icing sugar into a bowl and stir in the orange juice and rind. Add the melted chocolate and brandy and mix together until thoroughly combined. Spread the chocolate mixture evenly over the biscuit layer. Cover with clingfilm and chill for at least 4 hours.

4 Remove the cheesecake from the refrigerator, turn out onto a serving platter and decorate with chocolate leaves. Serve immediately.

white chocolate cheesecake

serves 8

base
- 55 g/2 oz butter
- 200 g/7 oz digestive biscuits, crushed
- 85 g/3 oz chopped walnuts

filling
- 450 g/1 lb mascarpone cheese
- 2 eggs, beaten
- 3 tbsp caster sugar
- 250 g/9 oz white chocolate, broken into pieces
- 300 g/10½ oz strawberries, hulled and quartered

topping
- 175 g/6 oz mascarpone cheese
- 50 g/1¾ oz white chocolate shavings
- 4 strawberries, halved

1 Preheat the oven to 150°C/300°F/Gas Mark 2. Melt the butter in a saucepan over a low heat and stir in the crushed biscuits and nuts. Spoon into a 23-cm/9-inch round springform cake tin and press evenly over the base with the back of a spoon. Set aside.

2 To make the filling, beat the mascarpone cheese in a bowl until smooth, then beat in the eggs and sugar. Melt the white chocolate in a heatproof bowl set over a saucepan of gently simmering water, stirring until smooth. Remove from the heat and leave to cool slightly, then stir into the cheese mixture. Stir in the strawberries.

3 Spoon the mixture into the cake tin, spread out evenly and smooth the surface. Bake in the preheated oven for 1 hour, or until the filling is just firm. Turn off the oven and leave the cheesecake to cool inside with the door slightly ajar until completely cold. Transfer to a serving plate.

4 For the topping, spread the mascarpone cheese on top. Decorate with the chocolate shavings and the strawberry halves.

Mmmm...
small bites & drinks

chocolate truffles

makes 40–50

- 350 g/12 oz plain chocolate, broken into pieces
- 115 g/4 oz butter
- 400 ml/14 fl oz double cream
- 1 tbsp vanilla extract
- grated coconut, cocoa powder, icing sugar, sifted, and chopped nuts, for coating

1 Put the chocolate, butter and double cream in a heatproof bowl set over a saucepan of gently simmering water and stir continuously. Stir in the vanilla extract, mix well and pour into a shallow dish. Leave the mixture in a refrigerator until firm enough to roll into balls.

2 Once the chocolate mixture has set, remove from the refrigerator and, working quickly, form small balls out of the chocolate by scooping it out with a melon baller.

3 Place the grated coconut, cocoa powder, icing sugar and chopped nuts on separate plates and roll the chocolate balls in the various coatings.

4 Place on a baking tray lined with baking paper, cover and chill until ready to serve.

italian chocolate truffles

makes 24

- 175 g/6 oz plain chocolate, broken into pieces
- 2 tbsp amaretto or orange liqueur
- 3 tbsp butter
- 4 tbsp icing sugar
- 50 g/1¾ oz ground almonds
- 50 g/1¾ oz milk chocolate, grated

1 Melt the plain chocolate with the amaretto in a heatproof bowl set over a saucepan of gently simmering water, stirring until well combined.

2 Add the butter and stir until it has melted. Stir in the icing sugar and the ground almonds.

3 Leave the mixture in a cool place until firm enough to roll into 24 balls.

4 Place the grated chocolate on a plate and roll the truffles in the chocolate to coat them.

5 Place the truffles in paper sweet cases and chill.

white chocolate truffles

makes 20

- 2 tbsp butter
- 5 tbsp double cream
- 225 g/8 oz Swiss white chocolate, broken into pieces
- 1 tbsp orange liqueur (optional)
- 100 g/3½ oz white chocolate, broken into pieces, for coating

1 Line a Swiss roll tin with baking paper.

2 Place the butter and cream in a small saucepan and bring slowly to the boil, stirring constantly. Boil for 1 minute, then remove from the heat.

3 Add the chocolate to the cream. Stir until melted, then beat in the liqueur, if using.

4 Pour into the prepared tin and chill for about 2 hours until firm enough to make into 20 balls. Chill the balls for an additional 30 minutes.

5 To finish, put the white chocolate in a heatproof bowl set over a saucepan of gently simmering water until melted. Dip the balls in the chocolate, letting the excess drip back into the bowl. Place on non-stick baking paper, swirl the chocolate with the tines of a fork, and let it harden.

nutty chocolate clusters

makes 30

- 175 g/6 oz white chocolate, broken into pieces
- 100 g/3½ oz digestive biscuits
- 100 g/3½ oz macadamia nuts or Brazil nuts, chopped
- 25 g/1 oz stem ginger, chopped (optional)
- 175 g/6 oz plain chocolate, broken into pieces

1 Line a baking tray with baking paper. Put the white chocolate in a large heatproof bowl set over a saucepan of gently simmering water and stir until melted.

2 Break the digestive biscuits into small pieces. Stir the crumbs into the melted chocolate with the chopped nuts, and stem ginger if using.

3 Place heaped teaspoons of the mixture on the prepared baking tray.

4 Chill the mixture until set, then remove from the baking paper.

5 Melt the plain chocolate as above and let it cool slightly. Dip the clusters into the melted chocolate, allowing the excess to drip back into the bowl. Return the clusters to the baking tray and chill in the refrigerator until set.

chocolate marshmallow fudge

makes 35–40 pieces

- 70 g/2½ oz butter, plus extra for greasing
- 115 g/4 oz plain chocolate, broken into pieces
- 200 g/7 oz white mini marshmallows
- 2 tsp water
- 115 g/4 oz blanched almonds, roughly chopped

1 Lightly grease a 20-cm/8-inch square cake tin.

2 Put the chocolate in a heatproof bowl set over a saucepan of gently simmering water and stir until the chocolate has melted. Put the marshmallows, butter and water in a large, heavy-based saucepan and gently heat, stirring frequently, until melted.

3 Remove the saucepan from the heat and pour the chocolate into the marshmallow mixture. Add the almonds and stir until well mixed.

4 Pour the mixture into the prepared tin. Tip the fudge out on to a chopping board and cut into squares. Chill until set.

rich chocolate fudge

makes about 50 pieces
- 85 g/3 oz butter, plus extra for greasing
- 450 g/1 lb sugar
- 150 ml/5 fl oz evaporated milk
- 150 g/5½ oz plain chocolate, broken into pieces
- 2 tbsp cocoa powder

1 Grease and line an 18-cm/7-inch square cake tin. Place all the ingredients in a large saucepan and heat gently, stirring over a low heat until the sugar dissolves and the chocolate melts to form a smooth mixture.

2 Bring to the boil and boil for 10–15 minutes, stirring occasionally. Pour into the prepared tin and smooth the top. Chill until firm.

3 Tip the fudge out on to a chopping board and cut into squares. Chill until set.

brazil nut brittle

makes 20

- sunflower oil, for brushing
- 350 g/12 oz plain chocolate, broken into pieces
- 100 g/3½ oz shelled Brazil nuts, chopped
- 175 g/6 oz white chocolate, roughly chopped
- 175 g/6 oz fudge, roughly chopped

1 Brush the bottom of a 20-cm/8-inch square cake tin with oil and line with baking paper. Put half the plain chocolate in a heatproof bowl and set over a saucepan of gently simmering water. Stir until melted, then spread in the prepared tin.

2 Sprinkle with the chopped Brazil nuts, white chocolate and fudge. Melt the remaining plain chocolate pieces and pour over the top.

3 Let the brittle set, then break up into jagged pieces using the tip of a strong knife.

chocolate cherries

makes 24

- 12 glacé cherries
- 2 tbsp dark rum or brandy
- 250 g/9 oz marzipan
- 125 g/4½ oz plain chocolate, broken into pieces
- milk, plain or white chocolate, to decorate (optional)

1 Line a baking tray with a sheet of baking paper.

2 Cut the cherries in half and place in a small bowl. Add the rum and stir to coat. Leave the cherries to soak for at least 1 hour, stirring occasionally.

3 Divide the marzipan into 24 pieces and roll each piece into a ball. Press half a cherry into the top of each marzipan ball.

4 Put the chocolate in a heatproof bowl set over a saucepan of gently simmering water. Stir until all the chocolate has melted.

5 Dip each marzipan ball into the melted chocolate using a cocktail stick, letting the excess drip back into the bowl. Place the coated cherries on the prepared baking tray and chill until set.

6 To decorate, melt a little extra chocolate and drizzle it over the top of the coated cherries. Leave to set.

chocolate creams

makes about 30

- 200 g/7 oz plain chocolate, broken into pieces
- 2 tbsp single cream
- 225 g/8 oz icing sugar
- cocoa powder, for dusting

1 Line a baking tray with baking paper. Melt 55 g/2 oz of the chocolate in a large heatproof bowl set over a saucepan of gently simmering water. Stir in the cream and remove the bowl from the heat.

2 Sift the icing sugar into the melted chocolate then, using a fork, mix together well. Knead to form a firm, smooth, pliable mixture.

3 Lightly dust a work surface with cocoa powder, turn out the mixture, and roll out to a 5-mm/¼-inch thickness, then cut into rounds, using a 2.5-cm/1-inch plain round cutter.

4 Transfer to the prepared baking tray and leave to stand for about 12 hours, or overnight, until set and dry.

5 When the chocolate creams have set, line a baking tray with baking paper. Melt the remaining chocolate in a heatproof bowl set over a saucepan of gently simmering water. Using 2 forks, carefully dip each chocolate cream into the melted chocolate. Lift it out quickly, letting any excess chocolate drain against the side of the bowl, and place on the prepared baking tray. Leave to set.

mini florentines

makes 20–30 florentines

- 75 g/2¾ oz butter
- 75 g/2¾ oz caster sugar
- 25 g/1 oz sultanas or raisins
- 25 g/1 oz glacé cherries, chopped
- 25 g/1 oz crystallized stem ginger, finely chopped
- 25 g/1 oz sunflower seeds
- 100 g/3½ oz flaked almonds
- 2 tbsp double cream
- 175 g/6 oz plain or milk chocolate, broken into pieces

1 Preheat the oven to 180°C/350°F/Gas Mark 4. Line 2 baking trays with baking paper. Place the butter in a small saucepan and melt over a low heat. Add the sugar, stir until dissolved, then bring to the boil. Remove from the heat and stir in the sultanas, glacé cherries, crystallized ginger, sunflower seeds and almonds. Mix well, then beat in the cream.

2 Place small, well-spaced teaspoons of mixture onto the prepared baking trays. Bake in the preheated oven for 10–12 minutes, or until light golden in colour. Remove from the oven and, while still hot, use a circular biscuit cutter to pull in the edges to form perfect circles. Leave to cool and turn crisp before removing from the baking trays.

3 Put the chocolate in a heatproof bowl set over a saucepan of gently simmering water and stir until melted. Spread most of the chocolate onto a sheet of baking paper. When the chocolate is on the point of setting, place the biscuits flat-side down on the chocolate and let it harden completely.

4 Cut around the florentines and remove from the baking paper. Spread the remaining chocolate on the coated side of the florentines, using a fork to mark waves. Leave to set.

chocolate pistachio biscotti

makes 24

- 25 g/1 oz butter, plus extra for greasing
- 175 g/6 oz plain chocolate, broken into pieces
- 350 g/12 oz self-raising flour, plus extra for dusting
- 1½ tsp baking powder
- 85 g/3 oz caster sugar
- 70 g/2½ oz polenta
- finely grated rind of 1 lemon
- 2 tsp amaretto
- 1 egg, beaten
- 115 g/4 oz pistachio nuts, roughly chopped
- icing sugar, sifted, for dusting

1 Preheat the oven to 160°C/325°F/Gas Mark 3. Grease a baking tray.

2 Put the butter and chocolate in a heatproof bowl set over a saucepan of gently simmering water. Stir over a low heat until melted and smooth. Remove from the heat and cool slightly.

3 Sift the flour and baking powder into a bowl and mix in the caster sugar, polenta, lemon rind, amaretto, egg and pistachio nuts. Stir in the chocolate mixture and mix to a soft dough.

4 Lightly dust your hands with flour, divide the dough in half and shape each piece into a 28-cm/11-inch long cylinder. Transfer the cylinders to the prepared baking tray and flatten with the palm of your hand to about 2 cm/¾ inch thick. Bake in the preheated oven for about 20 minutes, until firm to the touch.

5 Remove the baking tray from the oven and leave to cool. When cool, put the cylinders on a chopping board and slice them diagonally into thin biscuits. Return them to the baking tray and bake for a further 10 minutes, until crisp. Remove from the oven and transfer to wire racks to cool. Dust lightly with icing sugar.

chocolate liqueurs

makes 40
- 100 g/3½ oz plain chocolate, broken into pieces
- 20 glacé cherries or 20 hazelnuts or macadamia nuts

filling
- 150 ml/5 fl oz double cream
- 2 tbsp icing sugar
- 4 tbsp liqueur

to decorate
- 50 g/1¾ oz plain chocolate, melted
- marbled chocolate caraque

1 Line a baking tray with baking paper. Put the plain chocolate in a heatproof bowl and set over a saucepan of gently simmering water. Stir until melted. Spoon the chocolate into 40 paper sweet cases, spreading up the sides with a spoon or brush. Place upside down on the baking tray and leave to set.

2 Carefully peel away the paper cases. Place a cherry or nut in each cup.

3 To make the filling, place the double cream in a mixing bowl and sift the icing sugar on top. Whisk the cream until it is just holding its shape, then whisk in the liqueur.

4 Place the cream in a piping bag fitted with a 1-cm/½-inch plain nozzle and pipe a little into each chocolate case. Leave to chill for 20 minutes.

5 To decorate, spoon the plain chocolate over the cream to cover it. Add the caraque and let it harden.

ladies' kisses

makes 20

- 175 g/6 oz butter
- 115 g/4 oz caster sugar
- 1 egg yolk
- 100 g/3½ oz ground almonds
- 175 g/6 oz plain flour
- 55 g/2 oz plain chocolate, broken into pieces

1 Line 3 baking sheets with baking paper. Cream the butter and sugar together until pale and fluffy. Beat in the egg yolk, then beat in the almonds and flour. Continue beating until thoroughly mixed. Shape the dough into a ball, wrap in clingfilm and chill in the refrigerator for 1½–2 hours.

2 Preheat the oven to 160°C/325°F/Gas Mark 3. Unwrap the dough, break off walnut-sized pieces and roll them into balls between the palms of your hands. Place the dough balls on the prepared baking sheets, allowing space for the biscuits to spread during cooking. You may need to cook them in batches. Bake in the preheated oven for 20–25 minutes, until golden. Carefully transfer the biscuits to wire racks to cool.

3 Melt the chocolate in a heatproof bowl set over a saucepan of gently simmering water. Spread the melted chocolate on the flat sides of the cookies and sandwich them together in pairs. Return to the wire racks to cool.

chocolate crispy bites

makes 16

white layer

- 55 g/2 oz butter, plus extra for greasing
- 1 tbsp golden syrup
- 150 g/5½ oz white chocolate, broken into small pieces
- 50 g/1¾ oz toasted rice cereal

dark layer

- 55 g/2 oz butter
- 2 tbsp golden syrup
- 125 g/4½ oz plain chocolate, broken into small pieces
- 75 g/2¾ oz toasted rice cereal

1 Grease a 20-cm/8-inch square cake tin and line with baking paper.

2 To make the white layer, melt the butter, golden syrup and white chocolate in a bowl set over a saucepan of gently simmering water. Remove from the heat and stir in the rice cereal until it is well combined. Press into the prepared tin and smooth the surface.

3 To make the dark layer, melt the butter, golden syrup and plain chocolate in a bowl set over a saucepan of gently simmering water. Remove from the heat and stir in the rice cereal. Pour over the hardened white chocolate layer, leave to cool, then chill until hardened.

4 Turn out of the cake tin and cut into small squares using a sharp knife.

real hot chocolate

serves 1-2
- 40 g/1½ oz plain chocolate, broken into pieces
- 300 ml/10 fl oz milk
- milk chocolate curls, to decorate

1 Place the chocolate in a large, heatproof jug. Place the milk in a heavy-based saucepan and bring to the boil. Pour about one-quarter of the milk on to the chocolate and leave until the chocolate has softened.

2 Whisk the milk and chocolate mixture until smooth. Return the remaining milk to the heat and return to the boil, then pour on to the chocolate, whisking constantly.

3 Pour into warmed mugs or cups and decorate with chocolate curls. Serve immediately.

hot chocolate float

serves 4

- 450 ml/16 fl oz milk
- 225 g/8 oz plain chocolate
- 2 tbsp caster sugar
- 8 scoops coconut
  ice cream
- 8 scoops plain chocolate
  ice cream
- whipped cream,
  to decorate

1 Pour the milk into a saucepan. Break the chocolate into small pieces and add to the saucepan with the sugar. Stir over a low heat until the chocolate has melted, the sugar has dissolved and the mixture is smooth. Remove the saucepan from the heat.

2 Put 1 scoop of coconut ice cream into each of 4 heatproof glasses, top with a scoop of chocolate ice cream, then repeat the layers.

3 Pour the chocolate-flavoured milk into the glasses, top with whipped cream and serve immediately.

marshmallow float

serves 4
- 225 g/8 oz plain chocolate, broken into pieces
- 900 ml/1½ pints milk
- 3 tbsp caster sugar
- 8 marshmallows

1 Finely chop the chocolate with a knife or in a food processor. Do not over-process or the chocolate will melt.

2 Pour the milk into a saucepan and bring to just below boiling point. Remove the saucepan from the heat and whisk in the sugar and the chocolate.

3 Pour into warmed mugs or cups, top with marshmallows and serve immediately.

mocha cream

serves 2
- 200 ml/7 fl oz milk
- 50 ml/2 fl oz single cream
- 1 tbsp brown sugar
- 2 tbsp cocoa powder
- 1 tbsp coffee syrup or instant coffee powder
- 6 ice cubes

to decorate
- whipped cream
- milk chocolate, grated

1 Put the milk, cream and sugar into a food processor and process gently until combined.

2 Add the cocoa powder and coffee syrup and process well, then add the ice cubes and process until smooth.

3 Pour the mixture into glasses. Top with whipped cream, scatter the grated chocolate over the drinks and serve.

cool minty chocolate

serves 4
- 600 ml/1 pint ice-cold milk
- 6 tbsp drinking chocolate powder
- 200 ml/7 oz single cream
- 1 tsp peppermint extract
- 6 scoops of chocolate-mint ice cream
- fresh mint sprigs, to decorate

1 Pour half the milk into a small saucepan and stir in the drinking chocolate powder. Heat gently, stirring constantly, until just below boiling point and the mixture is smooth. Remove the saucepan from the heat.

2 Pour the chocolate-flavoured milk into a large chilled bowl and whisk in the remaining milk. Whisk in the cream and peppermint extract and continue to whisk until cold.

3 Pour the mixture into 4 glasses, top each with a scoop of ice cream, decorate with a mint sprig and serve immediately.

chocolate milkshake

serves 2

- 150 ml/5 fl oz milk
- 2 tbsp chocolate syrup
- 400 g/14 oz chocolate ice cream
- milk chocolate, grated, to decorate

1 Pour the milk and chocolate syrup into a food processor and process gently until combined.

2 Add the chocolate ice cream and process until smooth. Pour the mixture into tall glasses and scatter the grated chocolate over the shakes. Serve immediately.

Index